THE TRUMP-KIM SUMMIT: OUTCOMES AND OVERSIGHT

HEARING

BEFORE THE

SUBCOMMITTEE ON ASIA AND THE PACIFIC

OF THE

COMMITTEE ON FOREIGN AFFAIRS
HOUSE OF REPRESENTATIVES

ONE HUNDRED FIFTEENTH CONGRESS

SECOND SESSION

JUNE 20, 2018

Serial No. 115–139

Printed for the use of the Committee on Foreign Affairs

Available: http://www.foreignaffairs.house.gov/, http://docs.house.gov,
or http://www.gpo.gov/fdsys/

U.S. GOVERNMENT PUBLISHING OFFICE

30–497PDF WASHINGTON : 2018

COMMITTEE ON FOREIGN AFFAIRS

EDWARD R. ROYCE, California, *Chairman*

CHRISTOPHER H. SMITH, New Jersey
ILEANA ROS-LEHTINEN, Florida
DANA ROHRABACHER, California
STEVE CHABOT, Ohio
JOE WILSON, South Carolina
MICHAEL T. McCAUL, Texas
TED POE, Texas
DARRELL E. ISSA, California
TOM MARINO, Pennsylvania
MO BROOKS, Alabama PAUL
COOK, California SCOTT
PERRY, Pennsylvania RON
DeSANTIS, Florida
MARK MEADOWS, North Carolina
TED S. YOHO, Florida
ADAM KINZINGER, Illinois
LEE M. ZELDIN, New York
DANIEL M. DONOVAN, JR., New York
F. JAMES SENSENBRENNER, JR.,
 Wisconsin
ANN WAGNER, Missouri
BRIAN J. MAST, Florida
FRANCIS ROONEY, Florida
BRIAN K. FITZPATRICK, Pennsylvania
THOMAS A. GARRETT, JR., Virginia
JOHN R. CURTIS, Utah

ELIOT L. ENGEL, New York
BRAD SHERMAN, California
GREGORY W. MEEKS, New York
ALBIO SIRES, New Jersey
GERALD E. CONNOLLY, Virginia
THEODORE E. DEUTCH, Florida
KAREN BASS, California
WILLIAM R. KEATING, Massachusetts
DAVID N. CICILLINE, Rhode Island
AMI BERA, California
LOIS FRANKEL, Florida
TULSI GABBARD, Hawaii
JOAQUIN CASTRO, Texas
ROBIN L. KELLY, Illinois
BRENDAN F. BOYLE, Pennsylvania
DINA TITUS, Nevada
NORMA J. TORRES, California
BRADLEY SCOTT SCHNEIDER, Illinois
THOMAS R. SUOZZI, New York
ADRIANO ESPAILLAT, New York
TED LIEU, California

AMY PORTER, *Chief of Staff*   THOMAS SHEEHY, *Staff Director*
JASON STEINBAUM, *Democratic Staff Director*

———

SUBCOMMITTEE ON ASIA AND THE PACIFIC

TED S. YOHO, Florida, *Chairman*

DANA ROHRABACHER, California
STEVE CHABOT, Ohio
TOM MARINO, Pennsylvania
MO BROOKS, Alabama
SCOTT PERRY, Pennsylvania
ADAM KINZINGER, Illinois
ANN WAGNER, Missouri

BRAD SHERMAN, California
AMI BERA, California
DINA TITUS, Nevada
GERALD E. CONNOLLY, Virginia
THEODORE E. DEUTCH, Florida
TULSI GABBARD, Hawaii

C O N T E N T S

Page

WITNESSES

LETTERS, STATEMENTS, ETC., SUBMITTED FOR THE HEARING

APPENDIX

THE TRUMP-KIM SUMMIT: OUTCOMES AND OVERSIGHT

WEDNESDAY, JUNE 20, 2018

House of Representatives,
Subcommittee on Asia and the Pacific,
Committee on Foreign Affairs,
Washington, DC.

The subcommittee met, pursuant to notice, at 2:00 p.m., in room 2172 Rayburn House Office Building, Hon. Ted Yoho (chairman of the subcommittee) presiding.

Mr. YOHO. Good afternoon.

The hearing will come to order. I'd like to thank everybody for being here today.

For years, this committee has held—has led the effort in constraining the threat of North Korea's nuclear belligerence. Congress has worked under successive administrations to pressure the Kim regime, and in conjunction with the administration in multilateral efforts, this has occasionally brought us to inflection points—opportunities to change the course of this stubborn conflict.

The United States has reached another of these crossroads. Just over 1 week ago, President Trump met with Kim Jong-un, the current scion of the dictatorial Kim dynasty.

The word "historic" has been endlessly used to describe the meeting and that much is true. The two countries have never conducted direct leader-level talks before, and regardless of how these talks resolve, we can all be grateful that we are further from conflict than we were at the end of last year, and I would guess, 2 months ago.

Just over 1 week ago, President Trump met with Kim Jong-un, as we talked about, but simply holding a summit is not an accomplishment by itself.

The administration has taken an important first step. But much work needs to be done. The joint statement that emerged from Singapore contains few specifics about how these talks will advance our ultimate goal—the complete, verifiable, and irreversible denuclearization of North Korea. The statement, as our witnesses will testify, is generally similar to many statements North Korea has agreed to in the past, while making no good-faith efforts toward ever giving up its nuclear weapons.

While North Korea agreed to nothing new, the United States took the unprecedented step to indefinitely suspend our joint military exercises with our ally, the Republic of Korea.

There has been widespread disappointment regardless of party or affiliation that the United States would make these concessions when North Korea's only track record is for cheating and double dealing.

Importantly, nothing would make China and Russia happier than for the United States to voluntarily scale back our strategic capabilities in northeast Asia.

The White House has given some assurance that halting these exercises won't affect readiness, and it's encouraging that Secretary Mattis and the Pentagon are behind the idea.

But Congress must ensure that our defensive options are not affected and that the exercises can resume at the first sign of trouble.

We must be vigilant against threats from elsewhere in Asia. Our enemies will try to use the ongoing talks to advance their own goals, which may be at odds with our own. China is already pressing for the premature end of sanctions when North Korea has taken no concrete steps and has already eased trade restrictions along their shared border.

The indefinite standoff between the United States and a nuclear North Korea is in China's strategic interest. We can't forget that Xi Jinping has broken his diplomatic standoff with Kim to maximize his influence in the ongoing talks.

He certainly wouldn't mind wiping out the progress that we have made, turning back the clock a year or 2 and maintaining control over the perpetual threat to the United States that he can modulate through economic leverage.

So today we start a new chapter in a long-running endeavor of this committee. Some aspects of Congress' role will stay the same.

Ranking Member Sherman and I have worked together to press the administration to go after sanctions evaders large and small. It'll be more important to maintain our sanctions pressure as these talks go on.

We have written the administration—there are no banks that are too big to sanction. Targeting these bad actors will only strengthen the administration's hand.

But the Singapore summit has left us with many questions about how the negotiations will proceed in any denuclearization process that will emerge.

Our objective today is to start formulating recommendations that we can make to the administration and identify priorities we must ensure are considered as these talks progress.

We are thankful to be joined today by an expert panel who will advance their discussions and we look forward to hearing from you.

[The prepared statement of Mr. Yoho follows:]

<u>The Trump-Kim Summit: Outcomes and Oversight</u>
Subcommittee on Asia and the Pacific
House Committee on Foreign Affairs
Wednesday June 20, 2018
Opening Statement of Chairman Ted Yoho

For many years, constraining the threat of North Korea's nuclear belligerence has been a primary focus of Congress's foreign policy, and a major part of the Foreign Affairs Committee's work. Congress has worked under successive administrations to pressure the Kim regime, and in conjunction with administration and multilateral efforts, this has occasionally brought us to inflection points—opportunities to change the course of this stubborn conflict. The United States has reached another of these crossroads.

Just over one week ago, President Trump met with Kim Jong Un, the current scion of the dictatorial Kim dynasty. The word "historic" has been endlessly used to describe the meeting, and that much is true. The two countries have never conducted direct, leader level talks before, and regardless of how these talks resolve, we can all be grateful that we're farther from conflict today than we were at the end of last year.

But simply holding a summit is not an accomplishment by itself. Those of us who work to protect the United States from Kim's belligerence outside the administration have been left with some reasons to worry.

The joint statement that emerged from Singapore contains virtually no specifics about how these talks will advance our ultimate goal – the complete, verifiable, and irreversible denuclearization of North Korea. In fact, the statement is generally similar to many statements North Korea has agreed to in the past, while making no good faith efforts towards ever giving up its nuclear weapons.

In fact, while North Korea agreed to nothing new, the United States took the unprecedented step of indefinitely suspending our joint military exercises with our ally the Republic of Korea. There's been widespread disappointment, regardless of party or affiliation, that the United States would make this concession when North Korea's only track record is for cheating and double-dealing.

Even worse, nothing would make China and Russia happier than for the United States to voluntarily scale back our strategic capabilities in Northeast Asia. The White House has given us some assurances that halting the exercises won't affect readiness, and it's encouraging that Secretary Mattis and the Pentagon are behind the idea—but Congress must ensure that our defensive options are not affected, and that the exercises can resume at the first sign of trouble.

We also need to be vigilant against threats from elsewhere in Asia. Our enemies will try to use the ongoing talks to advance their own goals, which may be at odds with our own. China is already pressing for the premature end of sanctions when North Korea has taken no concrete steps, and has already eased trade restrictions along their shared border. The indefinite standoff between the United States and a nuclear North Korea is in China's strategic interest.

We can't forget that Xi Jinping has broken his diplomatic standoff with Kim to maximize his influence in the ongoing talks. He certainly wouldn't mind wiping out the progress that we've made, turning back the clock a year or two, and maintaining control over a perpetual threat to the United States that he can modulate through his economic leverage.

So today, we start a new chapter in a long running endeavor of this Committee. Some aspects of Congress' role will stay the same—Ranking Member Sherman and I have worked together to press the administration to go after sanctions evaders large and small, and it will be all the more important to maintain our sanctions pressure as these talks go on.

But the Singapore Summit has left us with many questions about how the negotiations will proceed and any denuclearization process that will emerge. Our objective todays is to start formulating recommendations that we can make to the Administration, and identifying priorities we must ensure are considered, as the talks progress. We're thankful to be joined today by an expert panel who will advance this discussion.

Mr. YOHO. And with that, members present will be permitted to submit written statements to be included in the official hearing record.

Without objection, the hearing record will remain open for 5 calendar days to allow statements, questions, and extraneous material for the record, subject to length limitation in the rules, and the witnesses' written statements will be entered into the hearing.

I now turn to the ranking member for any opening remarks he may have.

Mr. SHERMAN. Thank you, Mr. Chairman. Thank you for holding these hearings and I appreciate that opening statement.

The question the people are asking is whether this was a win-win or Kim win. I think it's clear that it is a Kim win, but this is just the first inning, and it is possible that as this goes forward it could be a win-win situation.

Let us see what—and I've been considered a dove at the very edge of the pale of reasonableness by saying that these negotiations will be successful if we are able to monitor, freeze, and limit the nuclear program in North Korea and that we will not get CVID, at least not in my lifetime, and they tell me I am in good shape. I'll see.

So that—whereas everyone else in the foreign policy administration has said the CVID, which means complete irreversible verifiable demilitarization.

So although I've been considered a dove on that, this thing passes is way more dovish than I am. What did we give up? We gave up, first, a meeting with the President of the United States, in Asia, boosting the credibility of the regime.

Most importantly, I think, we, in effect, gave up sanctions, at least ratcheting those sanctions. For example, Mr. Chairman, you and I sent this letter—and without objection, I'd like to put it in the record.

Mr. YOHO. Without objection.

Mr. SHERMAN. Urging the administration—and this is dated May 9th of this year—to impose tougher sanctions particularly on the larger Chinese banks that have been given a pass.

This letter, to my knowledge had not been answered. But if Singapore is the answer, this letter is dead. We are not going to be sanctioning more. We are going to be sanctioning less.

We are not going to be making it hard for Kim to breathe. We are going to be letting our foot off his neck. That is a huge win for Kim.

And then, finally, and for reasons I do not understand, our President has branded the exercises—military exercises as provocative and as war games, and has suspended them, at least the big ones planned in August.

We—if training isn't important to the military, then perhaps the Armed Services Committee has it wrong and we can save many tens of billions of dollars by not doing training and not doing exercises. That is absurd.

While I am talking about exercises, what we need is exercises involving Japan, the United States, and South Korea, and we have to tell our allies to "get over it."

The Japanese can't say that they can be the third largest economy and yet will never do anything to protect South Korea, and South Korea can't say there were terrible wrongs done over 70 years ago and therefore they won't do exercises with Japan.

These two countries increase the burden on Americans, the cost to Americans, and the possible death of Americans by refusing to exercise together, and that—and what we need is the three countries working with exercises together.

What did we get out of this hearing or, rather, this summit? We did not get a freeze on the production of fissile material.

At Yongbyon, both the plutonium reactor and the enrichment centrifuges are working today. North Korea has more fissile material today than when the President went to Singapore, and they will have a little bit more by the end of this hearing.

There is an implicit freeze on testing. But you don't need to test nuclear weapons constantly once you have demonstrated that they work. North Korea has demonstrated that they work. Russia hasn't done a nuclear test since 1990. That doesn't make me sleep well, thinking that those weapons are unavailable for use should they, God forbid, be deployed.

What we need is for North Korea to declare all of its nuclear missile facilities, we need to send inspectors, and we need a freeze, and if we don't get then all we have is vague promises and a statement about a denuclearized Korean Peninsula that apparently means to the North Koreans that will happen when swords are beaten into plowshares and wherein the entire world gives up its military forces.

So I look forward to learning from our experts what we can do to turn this into a win-win, notwithstanding the outcome of the first inning.

I yield back.

Mr. YOHO. I thank the ranking member. Now we will turn to other members for opening statements.

Mr. Rohrabacher of California.

Mr. ROHRABACHER. Thank you very much.

Let me just say for the record that I am very pleased with our President and I think that when I look at what's going on now and especially in reference to what happened in Korea, forgive me if I say this, but it's sort of like Yogi Berra's "it's deja vu all over again."

Having spent time in the Reagan White House and watched the same unrelenting negativity that the Democrats were playing against Ronald Reagan, who now they won't admit that—seeing that he ended the Cold War—but at that time they did everything they could to cast aspersions and weaken America's position in dealing with a Soviet Government, which at that time was our primary enemy in the world.

In fact, Ted Kennedy, when Reagan was up for reelection, even went to Russia—the Soviet Union—and met with Andropov, who was the worst of all of their leaders—during the Cold War and tried to find and to work with him, how can we prevent Ronald Reagan from being reelected.

And this talk about collusion with Trump, which they have been unable to prove, and have been put up and treated Ted Kennedy,

after that episode, as if he was some kind of a hero, is really dis-
concerting for those who know history and have been here for a
while.

But now we have a President that's trying to bring peace to
Korea. My father fought in Korea. He fought in Korea before I was
born. Actually, I was born in 1947. So he fought in Korea when I
was 5 years old, all right. But I remember when I was coming back
from a little stint in Vietnam when I was 19 and he told me how
chaotic the situation was in Korea and how many people's lives
were being lost.

Years later, he told me he could not believe that after all those
years we had not brought peace to Korea, with all of the loss of life
of the Americans.

Well, let me just put it this way. This President has made more
progress toward bringing peace to the Korean Peninsula than any
other President, any other American leader, in our own lifetime.

We should be proud of him and we should—it should be unacceptable that this unrelenting hostility and negativity to the point
that foreigners look at us and believe that the Democratic Party is
trying to wish that our President didn't succeed in this peace effort.
That's how loud and aggressive and unacceptable that criticism has
been.

We should be applauding our President now for what he's down
with Kim because he's opened the door—doesn't mean he's succeeded—but he's opened the door, just like Reagan opened the door
with the Soviet Union and many of the tactics he's used have been
the same.

So I appreciate that. Three cheers for our President and what
he's done with Korea.

Mr. YOHO. Appreciate your comments, and we pride ourselves on
being bipartisan on this committee, and we are going to have bipartisan discussions, as you can hear today.

We next go to Mr. Bera—Dr. Bera—from California.

Mr. BERA. Thank you, Mr. Chairman.

And I appreciate my colleagues. I wasn't in Congress when—I
think I was in high school when President Reagan was, you know,
addressing the Cold War. In hindsight, you know what? I am
happy that the Cold War ended and President Reagan deserves a
lot of credit for that.

I also know someone who's traveled to the Korean Peninsula
three times in the last 10 months who had breakfast with the vice
foreign minister yesterday from Korea.

Look, I'll give kudos to President Trump for engaging in dialogue. You know, Madeleine Albright said you don't have to like the
person sitting across the table from you but you have to be willing
to start a conversation and a dialogue, and that conversation has
started.

The devil now is in the details and, you know, the Republic of
Korea and the United States, there is no space between how we are
viewing this dialogue.

We are going to be very tough and, you know, I think the President and, hopefully, the administration will be as tough, walking
hand in hand, with our Korean allies.

The end goal here is denuclearization in a verifiable manner, and I am not ready to say I trust Kim Jong-un. I think we can look back on, you know, prior agreements and prior breaking of those agreements.

But we shouldn't be afraid to engage in a dialogue and move forward, and we should do so with our eyes wide open. We should, you know, stick to that end goal of a verifiable denuclearized Korea.

It may take time, as opposed to hastily rushing through things for an election cycle or political gain. Let's get this right, and it shouldn't be Democratic or Republican. This is about the United States of America and creating a more peaceful world.

Mr. YOHO. Thank you for your comments.

We will next go to Mr. Adam Kinzinger.

Mr. KINZINGER. Thank you, Mr. Chairman. I'll keep it to a minute.

Let me just say there is a DIME thing for getting things done—diplomatic, information, military, and economic.

When you're working against an adversary, the economic and especially the military piece is super important to back up the diplomatic piece, and this is where we are at. We are at the diplomatic part right now.

But the important part to see success on that is to continue to keep the economic pressure up and to continue to have viable and strong and aggressive military action if necessary. It is that military piece that will compel a diplomatic solution and it is that economic piece that will create enough pain to also compel a solution.

So as we go down however long this process is, and we are going to continue to do oversight of it, it is important that we not let up on those things that force us to the table in the first place, to continue to march down to a successful conclusion and I wish—I know left and right, Democrats and Republicans, wish this President luck to get it done. We certainly hope so.

And I yield back.

Mr. YOHO. Thank you for your comments.

Next, we will go to Mr. Gerry Connolly from Virginia.

Mr. CONNOLLY. Thank you, Mr. Chairman, and welcome to our panel.

I just want to say all of us hope that talking directly to North Korea will have payoff, and that payoff, as set by the President, has to be absolute denuclearization absolutely verifiable.

I believe that's a standard that will not be met. I believe that we have approached this in a naive way in which Kim Jong-un has gotten all the benefits and we have gotten nothing.

I hope that can be reversed. I hope we can ultimately get what it is we seek. But to be naive and to develop amnesia about the history of negotiations—denuclearization negotiations with North Korea is dangerous for the peninsula and puts everybody, North and South and the Sea of Japan, at risk.

So the stakes are very high here and the expectations have been set by the President in ripping up the Iran nuclear agreement, which wasn't good enough, even though it was working.

Well, we don't have anything working with respect to North Korea, other than a handshake and photo op. I hope to see and expect much more.

I yield back.

Mr. YOHO. Thank you.

Next, we will go to Ann Wagner from Missouri.

Mrs. WAGNER. Thank you, Mr. Chairman. Pardon me.

I appreciate this hearing on the Trump-Kim summit and I want to thank our witnesses for being here today.

I was in the Korean Peninsula last August in kind of the height of North Korea's belligerence and I met with South Korean President Moon Jae-in, and we discussed our shared hope for a peaceful resolution to last summer's ballistic missile test.

We have made tremendous progress since then, trading in threats for talks, and I believe there is real and genuine hope that we can move toward denuclearization.

I understand full well the history of the 1994 agreed framework, the Six-Party Talks, and the Leap Day agreement. So, of course, the U.S. cannot grant concessions without tangible steps toward Denuclearization and threat reduction.

But negotiations with the Kim regime are a serious opportunity to reduce the risk of war in the Asia Pacific and I look forward to tangible outcomes as the two parties continue negotiations.

I yield back.

Mr. YOHO. Thank you for your comments.

And here we are. We are getting ready to have you guys. Welcome to the Trump-Kim summit outcomes and oversight and—okay.

And before we get into that, Mr. Chabot has a comment he wants to make.

Mr. CHABOT. I'll be very brief. I wasn't going to talk but then I think I better.

For the last year and a half, many of the President's critics literally were warning that he was going to trigger World War III with respect to some of the aggressiveness toward North Korea.

He substantially ratcheted up the sanctions against North Korea along with the United States Congress and it actually worked to a considerable degree. We are not there yet, but I think it's heading in the right direction.

President Trump warned that, unlike previous U.S. administrations, both Democrat and Republican, North Korea would abandon its nuclear weapons.

Again, we haven't seen it actually happen yet. But I hope and pray that we are on our way because I think we all do want to avoid war, if at all possible.

So my advice to the President would be to keep the ratcheted-up sanctions in place. The nuclear weapons and his program has to go first before any of the sanctions are relieved. But we shouldn't trust this government in North Korea as far as we can throw them, as far as I am concerned.

They think nothing of starving and torturing and killing their own people and throwing them into gulags and just essentially forgetting about them.

So if you're going to do that to your own people, lying and cheating with an adversary—the United States and our allies, in this case—they won't think twice about that.

So we need to be very wary. That being said, I give President Trump great credit for surprising a lot of people who thought he was going to take us into war and may actually end up in peace for the region and the world, and that's what we hope happens.

I yield back.

Mr. YOHO. And I appreciate those comments and, you know, like I said, this is the Trump-Kim summit—the outcome's oversight—and as we were talking about earlier, so many of the things that you guys tell us goes into written form, whether it's resolutions or President—or letters to the President or to Treasury or to the State Department, and so I look forward to having your input, because we know what hasn't worked in the past.

And so I think it's time for outside of the box and this is pretty much outside of the box thinking and techniques, and, you know, people aren't familiar with that or used to that or comfortable with that.

We know, like I said, in the past what didn't work and we had career diplomats negotiating and negotiating, and here we are with the threat of a nuclear war on that peninsula further than we have ever been.

So we are thankful today to be joined by Mr. Bruce Klingner, who has been in front of this committee often, who is the senior research fellow for Northeast Asia at the Heritage Foundation Asia Studies Center.

Prior to working at the Heritage Foundation, Mr. Klingner served 20 years in the CIA in the Defense Intelligence Agency. Thank you for being here.

Dr. Mark Green, who is the senior vice president and Japan chair at the Center for Strategic and International Studies and director of Asian studies at the Edmund Walsh School of Foreign Service at Georgetown University.

Previously, he has also served on the staff of the National Security Council. Thank you for being here.

And Mr. Abraham Denmark, who is the director of the Asia program at the Woodrow Wilson International Center for Scholars. Prior to joining the Wilson Center, Mr. Denmark served as Deputy Assistant Secretary of Defense for East Asia and has held several positions in the U.S. intelligence community, and more importantly, another person here is Ms. Denmark, your mother, who's going to be watching you.

So we are expecting big things out of you. Thank you, ma'am, for being here.

And with that, you guys have been here enough. You know how the timer works. You know how the lights work. Press your button so we can hear you, and Mr. Klingner, go ahead. Thank you.

STATEMENT OF MR. BRUCE KLINGNER, SENIOR RESEARCH FELLOW FOR NORTHEAST ASIA, ASIAN STUDIES CENTER, THE HERITAGE FOUNDATION

Mr. KLINGNER. Thank you, Mr. Chairman, Ranking Member Sherman, and distinguished members of the panel.

It's truly an honor to be asked to appear before you again on such an important issue of national security. The U.S.-North Korea Summit was historic, and the first step of what would be a long process to cut the Gordian Knot of regime security threats to the United States and its allies.

Hopefully, this time is different. But it is a well-trod path that has previously led to disappointment. The summit was heavy on pomp and circumstance but light on substance. There was nothing new in the Singapore Communique, as you pointed out.

Each of the four major components was in previous accords with North Korea and were stronger or more encompassing in the previous iterations.

Most notably, the North Korean pledge to work toward complete denuclearization of the Korean Peninsula is weaker than the September 2005 Six-Party Talks joint statement.

And despite pre-summit statements by the administration that North Korea was moving toward accepting the U.N.-required concept of CVID, there was no evidence of that in the Communique.

The joint statement did not include any reference to missiles, BCW, verification, or human rights—all topics that the administration stated would be discussed during the summit.

Also of concern was President Trump's unilateral decision, without consulting our allies, to cancel what was deemed the "provocative" U.S.-South Korea "war games," terms that Washington had always rejected when North Korea used them.

This was a major unilateral concession to Pyongyang for which the U.S. received nothing in return. North Korea did not codify its nuclear and missile test moratorium in the Singapore Communique nor did Pyongyang reciprocate with a freeze of its own large scale annual winter and summer training cycles.

For years, the U.S. had correctly rejected North Korea's freeze for freeze proposal in which North Korea would suspend its prohibited nuclear missile tests in return for Washington and Seoul suspending the allied conventional military exercises.

As I wrote in 2015, canceling the combined exercises would degrade U.S. and South Korean deterrence and defense capabilities, necessitated by North Korea's previous attacks and threats.

Last week, my Heritage Foundation colleague, retired U.S. Army Lieutenant General Thomas Spoehr concluded that "canceling military exercises before North Korea has taken any concrete steps to demonstrate its intentions would be troubling. These exercises are necessary to ensure the interoperability and integration of operations and ensure readiness and preparedness."

General Spoehr assessed that "suspending these large joint exercises for an extended period of time, particularly for more than 6 months, could erode the readiness of U.S. and South Korean forces to successfully work together to defend South Korea. If the pledge by the President encompasses lower level exercises, the negative impact on readiness will be more immediate and severe."

Now, as we move forward, U.S. diplomats will now work to add meat to the bones of the Singapore Communique, and I'll summarize a few of the recommendations in my written testimony.

CVID—North Korea should unequivocally and publicly accept the U.N.-required abandonment of the regime's nuclear missile, and BCW programs in a complete, verifiable, and irreversible manner.

Require detailed, carefully-crafted text. Past negotiations with North Korea were flawed because the final agreement was short, vague, and didn't clearly delineate the definitions and responsibilities, as was the case with arms controls treaties with the Soviet Union and Warsaw Pact.

And the two sides differ over seemingly straightforward phrases such as "denuclearization" and the "Korean Peninsula."

We need to get it in writing. There has been a long history of American negotiators believing North Korea agreed to something based on our perception of a discussion or a verbal assurance by the regime. Oral agreements with North Korea are not worth the paper they are printed on. Distrust but verify. North Korean cheating on previous agreements makes it even more important to have more robust and intrusive verification regime than in the past, and again, I would point to the arms control treaties we had—START, INF, and CFE—with the Soviet Union as an example.

We need to maintain pressure until significant progress is achieved. U.S. negotiators should make clear the differences between negotiable trade sanctions such as constraints on resources, import and export of the U.N. resolutions, and nonnegotiable U.S.-targeted financial measures, which are law enforcement measures.

The North Korea Sanctions and Policy Enhancement Act Sections 401 and 402 allow the U.S. to suspend sanctions for up to 1 year or remove sanctions only if North Korea has made progress on several stipulated issues.

The U.S. and South Korea should not sign a peace treaty until the North Korean nuclear threat is eliminated and the conventional threat reduced. The North has extensive military forces along the DMZ and we should use measures such as those in the CFE treaty and the CSBM agreement to minimize that threat.

There should be no normalization of diplomatic relations without progress on human rights. The U.N. Commission of Inquiry concluded that North Korea's human rights violations were so widespread and systemic and egregious that they constituted crimes against humanity, and Kim Jong-un is on the U.S. sanctions list for human rights violations.

In conclusion, the U.S. and its allies must keep its shield up and its sword sharp until the threat necessitating their need is removed or reduced.

President John F. Kennedy declared the cost of freedom is always high, but Americans have always paid it. We share common values and common cause with our South Korean ally.

So yesterday, today, and tomorrow (foreign language spoken) "we go together." Thank you again for the privilege of appearing before you.

[The prepared statement of Mr. Klingner follows:]

The
Heritage Foundation

CONGRESSIONAL TESTIMONY

The Trump-Kim Summit: Outcomes and Oversight

Testimony before

Subcommittee on Asia and the Pacific of the

House Committee on Foreign Affairs

June 20, 2018

Bruce Klingner
Senior Research Fellow, Northeast Asia
The Heritage Foundation

214 Massachusetts Avenue, NE • Washington, DC 20002 • (202) 546-4400 • heritage.org

---

The Trump-Kim Summit: Outcomes and Oversight

Bruce Klingner

My name is Bruce Klingner. I am Senior Research Fellow for Northeast Asia at The Heritage Foundation. The views I express in this testimony are my own, and should not be construed as representing any official position of The Heritage Foundation.

A presidential meeting, particularly the first with an enemy nation, is considered the highest coin in the realm of diplomacy. Previous presidents felt that it wasn't worth spending on North Korea without clear evidence that the regime had committed to addressing allied security concerns. Such was the case in 2000 when President Bill Clinton turned down a summit invitation from Pyongyang because the regime refused to negotiate the terms of a missile agreement prior to the presidential visit.

What return on investment did the U.S. get from President Trump spending this valuable, once-in-a-lifetime presidential currency in a meeting with Kim Jong-un? The Singapore Communiqué was disappointing, particularly given the pre- and post-summit hype.

There was nothing new in the joint statement. Each of the four major components of the Trump-Kim communiqué were in previous accords with North Korea and most were stronger or more encompassing in previous iterations. Most notably, the North Korean pledge "to work toward complete denuclearization of the Korean Peninsula" in the Singapore Communiqué is weaker than the September 2005 Six Party Talks Joint Statement.

The Trump Administration emphasizes that the summit is only the beginning of a process. As such, it is the return to the first step in the well-trodden path of diplomacy with North Korea. Hopefully this time will turn out differently than the eight previous failed agreements with the regime.

Comparison of the Singapore Communiqué with previous North Korean agreements:

Singapore Communiqué: "The United States and the DPRK commit to establish new U.S.-DPRK relations in accordance with the desire of the peoples of the two countries for peace and prosperity.

- *October 12, 2000 - US-DPRK Joint Communiqué:* "The United States and the DPRK have decided to take steps to fundamentally improve their bilateral relations in the interests of enhancing peace and security in the Asia-Pacific region...[and] prepared to undertake a new direction in their relations."

Singapore Communiqué: "The United States and the DPRK will join their efforts to build a lasting and stable peace regime on the Korean Peninsula."

- *October 12, 2000 - US-DPRK Joint Communiqué:* "to reduce tensions on the Korean Peninsula and formally end the Korean War by replacing the 1953 Armistice Agreement with permanent peace arrangements."

Singapore Communiqué: Reaffirming the April 27, 2018 Panmunjom Declaration, the DPRK commits to work towards the complete denuclearization of the Korean Peninsula.

- *Treaty on the Non-Proliferation of Nuclear Weapons*: Article II - Each non-nuclear-weapon State Party to the Treaty undertakes not... to manufacture or otherwise acquire nuclear weapons or other nuclear explosive devices.
- *Joint Declaration of South and North Korea on the Denuclearization of the Korean Peninsula (1992)*: "South and North Korea shall not test, manufacture, produce, receive, possess, store, deploy or use nuclear weapons...South and North Korea shall not possess nuclear reprocessing and uranium enrichment facilities."
- *Six Party Talks Joint Statement (September 2005):*
    - The six parties unanimously reaffirmed that the goal of the six-party talks is the verifiable denuclearization of the Korean Peninsula in a peaceful manner.
    - The Democratic People's Republic of Korea (North Korea) committed to abandoning all nuclear weapons and existing nuclear programs and returning at an early date to the treaty on the nonproliferation of nuclear weapons (NPT) and to IAEA (International Atomic Energy Agency) safeguards.
- *Six Party Talks Joint Statement (February 2007)*
    - Within 60 days, North Korea will "Shut down and seal the Yongbyon nuclear facility for the purpose of abandonment; Invite the IAEA to return to the country to conduct all necessary monitoring and verification as agreed between the IAEA and the DPRK; Discuss a list of all its nuclear programs and materials, including the plutonium extracted from fuel rods that will be abandoned pursuant to the Joint Statement; and in the follow-on phase, the DPRK will provide a complete declaration of all nuclear programs and disablement of all existing nuclear facilities."

Singapore Communiqué: "The United States and the DPRK commit to recovering POW/MIA remains including the immediate repatriation of those already identified."

- *October 12, 2000 - US-DPRK Joint Communiqué:* "The U.S. side expressed appreciation for DPRK cooperation in recovering the remains of U.S. servicemen still missing from the Korean War, and both sides agreed to work for rapid progress for the fullest possible accounting."
- *Note:* U.S. teams previously operated in North Korea to recover and remove to the United States the remains of U.S. military personnel from the Korean War. Between 1995 and 2005, 33 recovery operations were conducted in North Korea and 200 sets of remains were returned.

Despite pre-summit statements by the administration that North Korea was moving toward accepting the UN-required concept of complete verifiable irreversible dismantlement of its nuclear programs, there was no evidence of that in the communiqué. When asked during a press conference why he didn't get Kim to agree to CVID, Trump replied, "Cause there's no time."

The Trump-Kim joint statement also did not include any reference to missiles, nuclear/missile test moratorium, biological and chemical weapons, verification, or human rights -- all topics that the Trump Administration stated would be discussed during the summit. By contrast, the 2000 President

---

Clinton-Marshal Jo communiqué included a pledge by North Korea to "not launch long-range missiles of any kind while talks on the missile issue continue."

Disparities Over Definitions

Resolving the difference between the U.S. and North Korea definitions of such seemingly straight-forward terms as "denuclearization" and "Korean Peninsula" is critical. Pyongyang defines "denuclearization" as global arms control and, as a self-professed member of the nuclear club, the regime will eliminate its nuclear arsenal when the other members do so.

In May, a senior North Korean official publicly rejected U.S. demands that the dictatorship rapidly, verifiably and irreversibly abandon its nuclear arsenal before getting any rewards. Instead, Vice Foreign Minister Kim Gye-gwan repeated long-standing demands for U.S. security and economic concessions in return for any constraint on Pyongyang's nuclear programs, and he affirmed that North Korea would not engage in unilateral disarmament.

Kim's statement was a reiteration of well-established regime positions that were well-known to Korea watchers but which surprised the White House which interpreted it as a broken promise. The realization of how far apart the two sides remained led the administration to lower expectations for the summit.

Another difference of view is that the U.S. interprets "Korean Peninsula" as the landmass encompassing North and South Korea. Therefore, denuclearizing the Korean Peninsula only pertains to the North Korean nuclear arsenal. However, Pyongyang defines the term to include anything that influences or impacts the peninsula which would include the U.S. extended deterrence guarantee ("nuclear umbrella") and any nuclear-capable system such as submarines, aircraft carriers, dual capable aircraft, and strategic bombers in Guam.

Because the U.S. and North Korea have such different interpretations and given the failure of eight previous diplomatic agreements with Pyongyang, it shows the necessity of having clearly delineated text and rigorous verification protocols. Both of those components were included in arms control treaties with the Soviet Union and Warsaw Pact but in none of the agreements with Pyongyang.

Canceling U.S.-South Korea Military Exercises

After concluding the summit with Kim Jong-un, President Trump held a press conference in which he unilaterally declared that he would cancel the "provocative" U.S. - South Korea "war games" -- terms that Washington had always rejected when used by North Korea. This was a major unilateral concession to Pyongyang for which the United States received nothing in return.

Trump described the routine training exercises as "inappropriate" while negotiating with North Korea, but focused more on their cost. He commented that the exercises are "tremendously expensive ... South Korea contributes but not 100 percent...We save money -- a lot" by canceling them.

During subsequent interviews. Trump affirmed that "I hated them from the day I came in. I said, why aren't we being reimbursed? We pay for it. We pay millions and millions of dollars for planes...It costs us a lot of money. I saved lot of money."

For years, the U.S. had correctly rejected North Korea's "freeze for freeze" proposal in which Pyongyang would suspend its prohibited nuclear and missile tests in return for Washington and Seoul suspending allied conventional military exercises. In September 2017, U.S. Ambassador to the UN Nikki Haley dismissed the freeze for freeze proposal as "insulting [since] "When a rogue regime has a nuclear weapon and an [intercontinental ballistic missile] pointed at you, you do not take steps to lower your guard."[1]

As I wrote in 2015, "canceling the combined exercises would have degraded U.S. and South Korean deterrence and defense capabilities necessitated by North Korea's previous invasions—terror attacks; its forward-deployed, offensively positioned military forces; and repeated threats of attacks, including nuclear strikes on the United States and its allies."[2]

Last week, my Heritage colleague U.S. Army Lieutenant General Thomas Spoehr (ret.) concluded that "canceling military exercises before North Korean has taken any concrete steps to demonstrate its intentions would be troubling...These exercises are necessary to ensure the interoperability and integration of operations [and] ensure readiness and preparedness."[3]

Spoehr assessed that "suspending these large joint exercises for an extended period of time, particularly for more than six months, could erode the readiness of U.S. and South Korean forces to successfully work together to defend South Korea. [If the president's pledge] "encompasses lower-level exercises, the negative impact on readiness will be more immediate and severe...Because ceasing these exercises would erode the U.S. and South Korea's ability to defend the peninsula."

Analysts at the Heritage Foundation have consistently recommended that the U.S. not accede to North Korean demands to cancel these exercises unless the north shows more tangible signs of seriousness in seeking peace and stability. Spoehr concludes that "the financial cost of these exercises is simply the price the U.S. must pay to defend its global national interests. The South Koreans pay their share of the exercise costs."

Alliances are the cost-effective option. A key component to mitigating risk in northeast Asia is through maintaining strong alliances and robust forward-deployed U.S. forces in the region. The Heritage Foundation's annual Index of Military Strength[4] highlights the importance of alliances to U.S. security.

An essay in the 2017 index explains:

---

[1] Paul D. Shinkman, " China's 'Freeze for Freeze' Plan for North Korea Gets Chilly Reception in U.S.," U.S. News and World Report, September 5, 2017, https://www.usnews.com/news/world/articles/2017-09-05/us-rejects-chinas-freeze-for-freeze-plan-for-north-korea.

[2] Bruce Klingner, " Respond Cautiously to North Korean Engagement Offers," The Heritage Foundation, April 20, 2015, https://www.heritage.org/defense/report/respond-cautiously-north-korean-engagement-offers.

[3] Thomas Spoehr, "Suspending Military Exercises in South Korea Carries Risks," The Heritage Foundation, June 12, 2018, https://www.heritage.org/asia/commentary/suspending-military-exercises-south-korea-carries-risks.

[4] "Index of U.S. Military Strength, The Heritage Foundation, https://www.heritage.org/military-strength.

> The costs of alliances, including the sometimes disproportionate cost of alliance leadership, must not be weighed against cash savings but rather against the cost of possible conflict in blood as well as treasure without them.

> Preserving peace and sustaining the global political and economic system's current U.S. orientation can be achieved most cost-effectively with allied support. The alternatives would call for either the maintenance of a huge U.S. military presence overseas far in excess of what is being maintained now or the holding of substantial forces in readiness at home in case the need arose to fight their way back into Europe or Asia to confront trouble in support of what is called "offshore balancing."[5]

Trump's decision was a mistake which risks degrading allied military deterrence and defense capabilities. He accepted the bad half of North Korea's bad freeze-for-freeze proposal without the regime codifying its nuclear and missile test moratorium in the Singapore Communiqué. Nor did Pyongyang reciprocate with a freeze of its own large-scale annual Winter Training Cycle and Summer Training Cycle conventional exercises.

It is unclear whether Trump will only cancel show-of-force activities such as flyovers of B-2 strategic bombers and large field training exercises Key Resolve and Ulchi Freedom Guardian or whether he will also ban unit field training exercises and command post exercises.

Even if restricted to large-scale exercises, the announcement could be a slippery slope in which Pyongyang demands curtailing additional allied military activity. North Korea has repeatedly criticized or taken action against an opponent which violated the regime's interpretation of a vague agreement. This year, North Korea canceled an inter-Korean meeting and criticized the allied military exercises that Kim Jong-un previously promised he wouldn't criticize because they "violated" the Panmunjom Declaration.

Trump's decision could also raise questions as to the continued utility of US Forces Korea on the peninsula if it cannot train there. Trump's unilateral decision, made without consultation with South Korea or Japan, will generate concerns of U.S. resolve and commitment to defend them. Japan Defense Minister Onodera told Secretary of Defense Mattis that Tokyo regretted not being informed beforehand of the decision, and that there are fears that the suspension of military exercises will weaken deterrence in the region. Onodera said, "US-South Korean military exercises are a critical pillar for regional peace and stability."[6]

Recommendations
The United States may have the opportunity to finally cut the Gordian Knot of intertwined issues of eliminating the North Korean nuclear threat to the U.S. and its allies, ending the Korean War with a permanent peace treaty, addressing the regime's atrocious human rights record, and establishing diplomatic relations with Pyongyang. Perhaps this time is different. But there is a long track record of previous failed diplomatic efforts with Pyongyang which were all greeted in their time as breakthroughs.

---

[5] Martin Murphy, "The Importance of Alliances for U.S. Security, The Heritage Foundation, https://index.heritage.org/military/2017/essays/importance-alliances-u-s-security/#fn10-3781.
[6] NHK News, June 16, 2018. https://www3.nhk.or.jp/news/html/20180616/k10011480201000.html (Japanese text).

As the U.S. and its allies work toward such an agreement, President Trump and U.S. diplomats should focus on several key tasks:

- *CVID.* North Korea should unequivocally, explicitly, and publicly accept the UN-required abandonment of the regime's nuclear, missile, and BCW weapons programs in a "complete, verifiable, and irreversible manner." [UN resolution cite]. It should be implemented in an expeditious manner.
- *Return to previous agreements.* Pyongyang should the affirm its recommitment to previous international denuclearization accords, the armistice ending the Korean War, the inter-Korean Basic Agreement, and return to the Non-Proliferation Treaty, the IAEA Safeguards agreement, and join the Missile Technology Control Regime.
- *Require detailed, carefully crafted text.* Past negotiations with North Korea were flawed because the allies, overeager to achieve an agreement, acquiesced to short, vague agreements which paid insufficient attention to details. Unlike extensively detailed arms control treaties with the Soviet Union which clearly identified definitions and provisions, all agreements with North Korea were terse and poorly crafted.
- *Create a Road Map.* Once both sides agree on what will be constrained and eliminated, there must be settlement on linkages and sequencing of responsibilities, as well as the timelines under which they will be carried out. There should be agreement on concise timelines for expedited rather than protracted implementation.
- *Get it in writing.* There has been a long history of Americans being surprised that North Korea had a different interpretation of the provisions and requirements of agreements. U.S. negotiator claims of oral agreements with North Korean counterparts enabled the regime to pocket concessions without reciprocating. Oral agreements with North Korea are not worth the paper they are written on. Unfortunately, we are already seeing signs of this in post-summit statements by President Trump and Secretary of State Pompeo.
- *Distrust but verify.* North Korean cheating on previous agreements makes it even more important to have a far more robust and intrusive verification regime than in the past. Parameters should be commensurate with the verification protocols of the START, INF, and CFE Treaties with the Soviet Union and Warsaw Pact.
  - o Provisions must include data declaration of North Korea's nuclear, chemical, biological and missile production, fabrication, test and storage facilities and the stockpile of fissile material and weapons of mass destruction arsenals; dismantlement of those facilities and destruction of the regime's WMD arsenals; on-site inspections of declared facilities; and short-notice challenge inspections of non-declared facilities. Given President Trump's criticism of the JCPOA, an NK deal must provide complete and total access to all North Korean military sites.
- *Maintain Pressure Until Significant Progress Is Achieved.* President Trump should not relax sanctions in return for North Korean pledges or minimalist implementation. Trump should make clear the differences between negotiable trade sanctions, such as U.N. measures that limit North Korean import of oil and export of coal (which can be relaxed in return for progress on denuclearization), from non-negotiable U.S. targeted financial measures, which are law enforcement measures defending the U.S. financial system.
  - o The North Korea Sanctions and Policy Enhancement Act, Sections 401 and 402 allow the U.S. to suspend sanctions for up to one year or remove sanctions only if North Korea has made progress on several stipulated issues. [North Korea Sanctions and Policy Enhancement Act of 2016, H.R. 757, 114th Cong., 2nd Sess., 2016.

- ***Peace treaty contingent on reducing conventional force threat.*** A peace treaty should be an endpoint of arms control negotiations rather than the opening gambit to improve relations with North Korea. Signing a peace treaty prematurely can dangerously degrade allied deterrence and defense capabilities since it would end the basis for the United Nations Command and could create momentum in both South Korea and the U.S. for "the war is finally over, bring the boys home."
    - The U.S. and South Korea should not sign a peace treaty until the North Korean nuclear threat is eliminated and the conventional threat reduced. North Korea has extensive conventional, mechanized, armor, and artillery corps deployed near the demilitarized zone, posing a threat to the south.
    - These forces should be capped and then weaned away from the forward area using measures similar to those in the Conventional Armed Forces in Europe Treaty and the accompanying Vienna Document of Confidence and Security Building Measures. Reducing the potential for either side to conduct a sudden-start invasion while increasing transparency on military forces can lower tensions by reducing the potential for miscalculation leading to a military clash.
- ***Economic assistance should be predicated on CVID progress.*** Provision of aid and assistance should be implemented in a manner to encourage economic reform, marketization, and the opening up of North Korea to the outside world rather than providing direct financial benefits to the regime.
    - Should be consistent with U.S. laws and lending requirements of International Financial Institutions. Executive Order 13722 bans "new investment in North Korea [and] any approval, financing, facilitation, or guarantee by a US person...where the transaction...would be prohibited...if performed by a United States person or within the United States."
    - There should be direct payments of wages to workers rather than the procedures in the Kaesong joint-economic experiment whereby wages were paid to the regime which siphoned off the money and provided trading scrib to workers to be redeemed in factory stores.
- ***No normalization of diplomatic relations without progress on human rights.*** Pyongyang's human rights violations have been so widespread, systemic, and egregious that the UN Commission of Inquiry determined they legally constituted "crimes against humanity." Some of the U.S. sanctions imposed on North Korea, including directly against Kim Jong-un, are due to human rights violations. Suspension or removal of U.S. sanctions are, in part, predicated on North Korea improving internal human rights conditions.[7]

Conclusion

The U.S. and its allies must keep their shield up and its sword sharp until the threat necessitating their need is removed or reduced. President John F. Kennedy declared, "The costs of freedom is always high -- but Americans have always paid it." America, and its mothers and fathers of those brave men and women in the U.S. military do not take that commitment lightly but we are willing to make it.

The parents of 28,500 American warriors have pledged their most precious treasure – their children – to defend our allies in the region. Many more would come if there were a crisis. There can be no

---

[7] North Korea Sanctions and Policy Enhancement Act, Sections 401 and 402, https://www.congress.gov/congressional-report/114th-congress/house-report/392/1?overview=closed.

stronger signal of American commitment. We share common values and common cause with our South Korean ally. Yesterday…today…and tomorrow….katchi kapshida ("we go together").

* * * * * * * * * * * * * * * * *

The Heritage Foundation is a public policy, research, and educational organization recognized as exempt under section 501(c)(3) of the Internal Revenue Code. It is privately supported and receives no funds from any government at any level, nor does it perform any government or other contract work.

The Heritage Foundation is the most broadly supported think tank in the United States. During 2014, it had hundreds of thousands of individual, foundation, and corporate supporters representing every state in the U.S. Its 2014 income came from the following sources:

Individuals 75%
Foundations 12%
Corporations 3%
Program revenue and other income 10%

The top five corporate givers provided The Heritage Foundation with 2% of its 2014 income. The Heritage Foundation's books are audited annually by the national accounting firm of RSM US, LLP.

Members of The Heritage Foundation staff testify as individuals discussing their own independent research. The views expressed are their own and do not reflect an institutional position for The Heritage Foundation or its board of trustees.

Mr. YOHO. Thank you for that.
Dr. Green.

STATEMENT OF MICHAEL J. GREEN, PH.D., SENIOR VICE PRESIDENT FOR ASIA, JAPAN CHAIR, CENTER FOR STRATEGIC AND INTERNATIONAL STUDIES

Mr. GREEN. Chairman Yoho, Ranking Member Sherman, and members of the committee, thank you for inviting me back this time to talk about the outcomes of the June 12th summit.

I hope I can add some clarity on what was achieved, what we failed to achieve, and what we may have unleashed in terms of broader geopolitics in Asia with this summit. In each of these areas I think there is an oversight role for Congress, which I will touch on in my remarks.

As several of the members of the committee have noted, Kim Jong-un has certainly achieved two of his objectives—first, he is now able to claim de facto U.S. recognition of this nuclear weapons status.

When I was in the White House under President Bush, the North Koreans wanted a summit with George W. Bush. They tried to get one with Bill Clinton. They tried to get one with Barack Obama.

Those Presidents said no because they thought the North Koreans were doing this to try to claim de facto status for their nuclear weapons.

Kim has checked that box. We can debate about whether it's worth it, but that's one accomplishment.

Second, as has been mentioned, Kim has successfully blunted sanctions. Not necessarily U.S. sanctions but China's imposition of sanctions. China counts for 90 percent of North Korean trade.

What did the United States achieve? North Korea has stopped testing ballistic missiles and nuclear weapons. Kim probably knows that if he resumes testing the President will put back together the maximum pressure of international coalition of sanctions, if not military options.

But we should also acknowledge that North Korea had violated every freeze in the past and could do so again at any time, and as others have mentioned on the committee, a freeze in testing is not a freeze in production and development of weapons and fissile material.

The language, as my colleague pointed out, in the June 12th summit falls far short of previous agreements. Kim's firm and unwavering commitment to complete denuclearization of the Korean Peninsula is a line I heard and saw in documents in many negotiations with the North.

When they say this, they mean we'll denuclearize when you denuclearize, meaning when you stop protecting Japan and Korea stop sanctions.

The North Koreans look at the nonproliferation treaty of 1968 with the U.S. and other nuclear power's promise to get rid of nuclear weapons and I think Pyongyang realizes that's what you say to get membership in the nuclear weapons club.

So like Mr. Klingner, I don't put much value on that particular statement. It's possible Secretary Pompeo will be able to produce more details than we've seen. I certainly hope so.

The pattern in the past has been for North Korea to prevaricate and not implement after the ink dries, and I think Congress can help Secretary Pompeo get more leverage in that difficult process.

We'll know it's different this time or potentially different if Secretary Pompeo can get the North Koreans to produce a statement on North Korea's full weapons and missile inventory and a verification plan.

We were supposed to get this in the Six-Party Talks I joined. They were supposed to be part of the agreed framework. Doesn't mean that they would go down that path but it's the first necessary step.

Absent real steps toward denuclearization of that kind, Congress would be right to insist on fuller implementation of sanctions including secondary sanctions against Chinese or Russian firms, and I would argue to do so before the September U.N. General Assembly when Kim Jong-un is expected to be addressing the international community.

Also, U.S. unilateral sanctions, while they're still on, are not a passive instrument. It takes active implementation. Is the administration going to do maritime interdiction operations when we catch the North Koreans transporting dangerous materials? Will they be imposing sanctions when they catch new banks?

I think Congress has an important role in pushing the administration not only to maintain sanctions but to actively implement them.

A second area requiring greater congressional oversight is management of our alliances. All of us who work in Asia were confused or disturbed by the President's abrupt cancellation of U.S. joint military exercises.

This was not a unilateral decision, if you were in Japan or Korea or Australia. This was a bilateral decision between North Korea and the U.S., proposed by China and Russia, with no consultation with our closest allies, compounded by the President's statement that someday he'd like to get out of Korea altogether.

I think most veterans of North Korea diplomacy, Republican or Democrats, would say they hope the President succeeds. We should give Secretary Pompeo the leverage he needs. But it probably won't work.

What we do know for sure is we are going to need our alliances. We'll especially need them if North Korea continues developing dangerous weapons.

We are also going to need our alliances because we are playing two games of chess in Asia right now. We are not just playing this game of chess with North Korea. We are playing a much more consequential long-term game with China about who's going to dominate the rules and security in this region.

On that chessboard, we make a mistake sending signals of lack of resolve or potential retreat on our alliances. I think the administration would be appreciative, perhaps, of Congress asking how this negotiation is going to advance the strategy that the President's own national security strategy and the national defense strategy articulate that we are in a competitive game with China.

How will our diplomacy with North Korea—how will our coordination with our allies help us in that other chess game, which is no less important to our security than what the President is trying to do with North Korea?

Thank you, and I look forward to your questions.

[The prepared statement of Mr. Green follows:]

CSIS | CENTER FOR STRATEGIC & INTERNATIONAL STUDIES

Statement Before the

House Committee on Foreign Affairs

Subcommittee on Asia and the Pacific

"The Trump-Kim Summit: Outcomes and Oversight"

A Testimony by:

Dr. Michael J. Green

Senior Vice President for Asia, Center for Strategic and

International Studies

Director of Asian Studies, Edmund A. Walsh School of Foreign

Service

Georgetown University

June 20, 2018

2172 Rayburn House Office Building

WWW.CSIS.ORG

1616 RHODE ISLAND AVENUE NW | TEL: (202) 887-0200
WASHINGTON, DC 20036 | FAX (202) 775-3199

Chairman Yoho, Ranking Member Sherman, I am pleased to speak before this committee on the outcomes of President Trump's June 12 Summit in Singapore with North Korean leader Kim Jong-un. I hope to add some clarity about what we have accomplished, failed to accomplish, and potentially unleashed in terms of the larger geopolitics of East Asia. There is an important oversight role for Congress in each of these areas which I will highlight in my remarks.

Kim Jong-un appears to have achieved two of his objectives with this summit. First, the summit allows him to claim *de facto* U.S. recognition of his nuclear weapons status. The North sought summits with Presidents Clinton and George W. Bush for this reason. Both Presidents understood the real purpose and refused, but now Pyongyang has checked that box. Second, Kim has succeeded in blunting and diluting the U.S. campaign of "maximum pressure"—at least in terms of China, which accounts for 90% of North Korean trade and has visibly backed away from full implementation of sanctions since the summit was announced.

What did the United States achieve? North Korea has stopped testing ballistic missiles and nuclear weapons. Kim Jong-un appears to be enjoying the international acclaim he is receiving. He probably realizes that a resumption of testing would allow the United States to reassemble the international coalition needed to return to maximum pressure. However, we must acknowledge that North Korea has violated testing freezes in the past and could do so again at any time. Moreover, a freeze in testing does not constitute a freeze in the regime's ongoing nuclear weapons development programs.

Kim Jong-un may be a new and different leader, but there is nothing in the June 12 Singapore Joint Statement that would constitute a new commitment by the North to denuclearization. In fact, the language in the June 12 Joint Statement falls far short of previous agreements. Kim's "firm and unwavering commitment to complete denuclearization of the Korean Peninsula" is a rehash of earlier North Korean language that Pyongyang has always conditioned on the United States first ending *its* security commitments to Japan and South Korea. This unhelpful language contrasts with the specifics of prior diplomatic agreements with North Korea:

- in the 1992 North-South Denuclearization accord the North committed to "not test, manufacture, produce, receive, possess, store, deploy or use nuclear weapons;"
- in the 1994 Agreed Framework the North pledged to allow full International Atomic Energy Agency safeguards and inspections;
- and in the 2005 Six Party Joint Statement the North committed to "to abandoning all nuclear weapons and existing nuclear programs and returning at an early date" to the NPT and to IAEA safeguards.

It is possible that Secretary of State Pompeo will produce more detailed plans in the weeks and months ahead, but the general pattern to date has been for North Korea to prevaricate and stall after the ink has dried on agreements – not to add more details for implementation. As we know, the North began cheating on the 1992, 1994 and 2005 agreements almost immediately by restarting reactors, embarking on clandestine uranium enrichment paths to nuclear weapons, or testing nuclear weapons.

We will know this time is different if Secretary Pompeo's team can compel their counterparts to produce a statement on the North's full weapons and missile inventory and to agree on verification protocols for inspections. This would not necessarily mean that the North intends to follow through, but it would represent a concrete step towards verifiable denuclearization that Pyongyang was supposed to have delivered in previous agreements. Alternatively, the North may turn over weapons or allow inspectors into a critical facility –but it would have to be considerably more than what we saw last month when the North invited friendly journalists to witness the pretend demolition of a collapsing test site. Absent real steps towards denuclearization, Congress would be right to insist on fuller implementation of sanctions, including secondary sanctions against Chinese or Russian firms, and to do so before Kim Jong-un embarks on his expected visit to address the UN General Assembly in September.

A second area requiring greater Congressional oversight is management of our alliances. The President's abrupt cancellation of U.S. joint military exercises with South Korea was a bombshell to our allies. It would be a mistake to call this a "unilateral" decision. It was, in fact, a *bilateral* decision reached with North Korea at the suggestion of China and Russia over the heads of our closest allies in the region. The shock to our alliances was compounded by the President's statement that he would like eventually to pull all U.S. troops out of South Korea. If you ask veterans of North Korea diplomacy from either party, the overwhelming majority would predict that Kim Jong-un is not going to denuclearize. This does not mean that we should abandon our current diplomatic path, but it does mean that we should be reinforcing our alliances to contain and deter a significantly more dangerous North Korea. Signaling a desire to retreat from the peninsula only encourages the North to think that its nuclear weapons can break our will and intimidate our allies.

A dismissive attitude towards our alliances also emboldens China. The President's 2018 National Security Strategy rightly identified great power competition with China and Russia as the central challenge to our security and our alliances as essential to meeting that challenge. As the U.S. Pacific Commander testified in Congress in April, China has a "clear intent to erode U.S. alliances and partnerships in the region." In recent years Beijing has pressured South Korea to sign a declaration opposing U.S. alliances in Asia –unsuccessfully --and has boycotted billions of dollars in South Korean products in an effort to stop U.S. missile defense deployments to the peninsula. Congress would be right to ask the administration how the June 12 summit will impact our ability to meet the challenges posed by China, which is no less important than the North Korea nuclear negotiations themselves. Indeed, the credibility of our alliances is one of the greatest sources of leverage we have to push both China and North Korea to do the right thing on the Korean peninsula.

Thank you.

Mr. YOHO. Thank you for your comments.
Mr. Denmark.

STATEMENT OF MR. ABRAHAM DENMARK, DIRECTOR, ASIA PROGRAM, THE WOODROW WILSON INTERNATIONAL CENTER FOR SCHOLARS

Mr. DENMARK. Chairman Yoho, Ranking Member Sherman, members of the committee, it's an honor to be invited to give testimony today to review last week's remarkable summit between President Trump and Kim Jong-un.

Before I begin, I would just like to emphasize that the views expressed in this testimony are mine alone and not those of the Wilson Center or the U.S. Government.

I am a strong supporter of diplomacy with North Korea. I work this challenge every day during my most recent appointment at the Department of Defense and I am deeply familiar with the risk associated with the military conflict with North Korea.

Still, we should remember that diplomacy is a tactic, not a strategy and certainly not an objective. While the diplomatic process that has begun—that has begun may yield results eventually, the unfortunate fact is that the United States got a bad deal in Singapore.

First, I would like to summarize what happened. The most geopolitically significant outcome of the summit was to set the U.S.-DPRK relationship——

Mr. CONNOLLY. Excuse me, Mr. Chairman. Could we ask Mr. Denmark to pull that mic closer to him? It's a little hard to hear you.

Mr. DENMARK. I apologize, sir.

Mr. CONNOLLY. Thank you.

Mr. YOHO. Not a problem. Thank you.

Mr. DENMARK. The most geopolitically significant outcome of the summit was to set the U.S.-DPRK relationship onto a diplomatic track.

Additionally, the President suspended major U.S.-ROK joint military exercises. This gave away a major piece of leverage while over time weakening the capabilities of our forces stationed in Korea for no appreciable gain.

I should add that I disagree with the President's characterization of these exercises as provocative. These exercises are stabilizing and defensive, and they are essential for deterrence, reassurance, and readiness.

This is not to say that military exercises are sacrosanct. Adjusting exercises should be part of a negotiation.

In any case, suspending exercises does not require the President denigrating their utility. There is also a lot that didn't happen in Singapore. Most importantly, North Korea made no new commitments toward denuclearization.

North Korea remains free to manufacture more nuclear weapons, ballistic missiles, and other weapons of mass destruction. There is no deadline for them to eliminate their illegal capabilities or even to freeze their continued production.

Further, as you can see in the chart I appended to my testimony, North Korea's denuclearization commitment made last week was the least specific commitment it has ever made.

Moreover, the joint statement from Singapore made no mention of verification. Considering North Korea's repeated history of violating past agreements, there is little reason to trust them this time.

I would point to four significant implications of the Singapore summit. One, despite the President's claims, North Korea remains a significant threat to the United States and our allies in East Asia.

North Korea has the same ability today to attack our allies and possibly the United States as it had before the President met Kim.

Two, the summit was a tremendous propaganda victory for Kim Jong-un. This is why previous Presidents have refused to meet with North Korean leaders. Doing so in itself is a major concession and conveys tremendous legitimacy to the North Koreans.

Three, the summit injected a new turbulence into U.S. alliances with Japan and the ROK. The President's effusive praise of Kim Jong-un and his willingness to meet with Kim and make significant concessions despite making so little progress on denuclearization inflamed allied concerns about U.S. reliability.

And four, China got everything it wanted. China has long sought for the United States to be committed to a diplomatic process and to suspend its military exercises in Korea.

To conclude, I would like to offer four points on next steps. On the first, time is not on our side. North Korea can continue to mass produce nuclear warheads and ballistic missiles as Kim Jong-un actually called for in his New Year's speech in January.

There is a danger that the U.S. has entered into an open-ended diplomatic process which would give North Korea a distinct advantage.

One way for the United States to address time pressures in this negotiation would be to achieve a complete freeze on North Korea's nuclear and ballistic programs as an early step in this process.

Second, to supplement the President's trust of Kim Jong-un, the U.S. should insist on strict inspection and verification regimes to accompany any concession North Korea may make toward denuclearization.

Third, the United States should prepare for increased friction with China over maintaining pressure on North Korea. I expect China will soften its enforcement of sanctions on North Korea and the United States should expect to be prepared to hold China accountable, even to the point of enacting secondary sanctions on China's entities that continue to do business with North Korea.

And fourth, considering the continued threat posed by North Korea, the United States should ensure that its military forces and alliances in the region remain ready and robust.

Any strategy toward North Korea is far stronger if the full weight of the United States and our allies can be brought to bear.

Further, the people of the U.S. military deserve the resources needed to do their job effectively and the ability to exercise as needed.

Readiness saves lives and ensures that our military remains the most awesome feared fighting force in the history of the world.

Going forward, we must remain clear-eyed about how we are dealing with. The threat from North Korea remains real and Kim is not to be trusted.

A credible high-quality deal will be very difficult to achieve and even more difficult to implement and verify. After the pageantry of Singapore, the difficult work of diplomacy and denuclearization still lies ahead.

Thank you, and I look forward to your questions.

[The prepared statement of Mr. Denmark follows:]

Wilson Center

Congressional Testimony

**Before the House Committee on Foreign Affairs
Subcommittee on Asia and the Pacific**

Hearing on "The Trump-Kim Summit: Outcomes and Oversight"

Abraham M. Denmark
Asia Program Director
Senior Fellow at the Kissinger Institute on China and the United States
Woodrow Wilson International Center for Scholars

June 20, 2018

Rayburn House Office Building Room 2172

Chairman Yoho, Ranking Member Sherman, members of the Committee, my distinguished fellow panelists: it is an honor to be invited to give testimony today to review last week's remarkable summit between President Trump and North Korean leader Kim Jong Un. Given what happened in Singapore – and what didn't happen – this hearing provides an opportunity for a valuable public discussion about a topic of critical importance.

My name is Abraham M. Denmark, and I am Director of the Asia Program at the Woodrow Wilson International Center for Scholars, where I also hold an appointment as a Senior Fellow in the Kissinger Institute on China and the United States. The views I express in my testimony are mine alone, and not those of the Wilson Center or of the U.S. government.

At the outset, I want to be clear that **I am a strong supporter of diplomacy with North Korea.** I worked the North Korea challenge every day in my time at the Department of Defense, and I am deeply familiar with the costs and risks that would be involved in a military conflict with North Korea. While I oppose taking military options off the table, I firmly believe that realistic diplomacy – complemented by sustained pressure as well as the resolve to demand reciprocal concessions from North Korea– is preferable to the risks of a potentially catastrophic conflict. As President Kennedy said, "let us never negotiate out of fear. But let us never fear to negotiate."

Still, while I believe in diplomacy, we should remember it is a tactic – not a strategy, and certainly not an objective. While entering into a diplomatic process with Pyongyang is a positive development, North Korea has so far received several significant concessions without giving much in return. In several ways the United States emerged from the Singapore summit at a greater disadvantage than when it began. **While the diplomatic process that has begun may yield results eventually, the unfortunate fact is that the United States got a bad deal in Singapore.**

What Happened in Singapore

Regardless of its outcome, a meeting between the President of the United States and the North Korean leader was undeniably historic. After over 70 years of hostility and multiple instances of extreme tension, the meeting of the two leaders offered a moment of hope despite all the skepticism, doubt, and distrust that infuses U.S.-DPRK relations. Despite the significant disappointment of the summit overall, it did have some tangible results.

- **The most geopolitically significant outcome of the summit was to officially set the U.S.-DPRK relationship onto a diplomatic track.** While it is unclear if this process will generate any tangible results, this is far better than the tension and "fire and fury" rhetoric from previous months.

- Though often overlooked, it is important to recognize that North Korea committed to recovering American POW/MIA remains, including the immediate repatriation of those remains already identified. While this is a positive gesture from Pyongyang, we should recall that they have in the past demanded payment for the return of our people's remains.

- **Unilaterally suspending major U.S.-ROK joint military exercises gave away a major piece of American leverage while over time weakening the capabilities of our forces stationed in Korea, for no appreciable gain.** North Korea is still free to conduct its major exercises, and its pledge to halt nuclear and missile tests was not included in the Singapore summit joint statement – meaning the president's concession appears entirely unilateral. Cancelling these exercises has been a long-held goal for North Korea and China, and the president adopted their argument when he called the exercises "provocative".[1] I disagree with the president's characterization. These joint military exercises are stabilizing and defensive, and they are essential for deterrence, reassurance, and readiness. They ensure that that U.S. and ROK forces are ready to "fight tonight" to defend against any potential aggression on the peninsula. The President often touts the power of the U.S. military – in the past, he has warned that U.S. military options are "fully locked and loaded" in Korea.[2] But the reality is that the only reason these forces are so ready to go is because they exercise regularly.

  This is not to say that military exercises are sacrosanct and should not be adjusted under any circumstance. Adjusting exercises should be part of a negotiation with North Korea - not a unilateral concession for which we get nothing in return. In any case, it does not require the president denigrating the utility of our exercises. Doing so suggests that exercises are primarily bargaining chips – not actions that are necessary to maintain military readiness – and will have global implications for exercises held all around the world.

What Didn't Happen in Singapore

---

[1] Jim Michaels, "U.S. will suspend military drills with South Korea, but they can be restarted quickly," *USA Today*, June 12 2018, https://www.usatoday.com/story/news/world/2018/06/12/trump-suspend-military-exercises-south-korea/693527002/.

[2] "Trump: military solutions 'locked and loaded' against North Korea threat," *Reuters*, August 11, 2017, https://www.reuters.com/article/us-northkorea-missiles-trump-idUSKBN1AR15M.

- **North Korea has made no new commitments to denuclearization, and in fact has backed away from its previous commitments.** In Singapore, Kim was able to simply reiterate the commitment made at Panmunjom in April, that "South and North Korea confirmed the common goal of realizing, through complete denuclearization, a nuclear-free Korean Peninsula."[3] North Korea remains free to manufacture more nuclear weapons, ballistic missiles, and other weapons of mass destruction – even though it has unilaterally frozen testing of its nuclear weapons and certain ballistic missiles. There is no deadline for them to eliminate their illegal capabilities, or even freeze their continued production.

  Further, as you can see in the chart I appended to my testimony, North Korea's denuclearization commitment made last week was the least specific commitment it has ever made. For example, in 2005 as a result of the 6-Party Talks process, North agreed to "verifiable" denuclearization and to "abandoning all its nuclear weapons and nuclear programs and returning, at an early date" to the NPT.[4] The reality is that the commitment Kim made last week is a significant downgrade from any of its previous commitments.

- **The joint statement from Singapore did not mention human rights, other weapons of mass destruction, ballistic missiles or verification, meaning the president could only point to his personal trust in Kim Jong Un.** Considering North Korea's repeated history of violating past agreements, there is little reason to trust them this time. Moreover, Kim rules a regime that commits systematic, widespread and gross human rights violations against his own people, and is believed to have directed acts of aggression against our ROK ally and the rapid acceleration of North Korea's nuclear and ballistic missile testing program upon taking power. Yet in the Singapore joint statement and in the president's comments since then, there has been no mention of verification or enforcement. Instead, the president has repeatedly described the trust he holds for Kim Jong Un. Time will tell if this trust is well placed, but I am skeptical about entrusting the future security of my country or our allies in the goodwill of Kim Jong Un.

- **Despite their pledge to completely denuclearize the Korean peninsula, Washington and Pyongyang have yet to agree on a common definition of denuclearization.** Without a common understanding of what is to be achieved, it is

---

[3] *Panmunjeom Declaration for Peace, Prosperity, and Unification of the Korean Peninsula*, April 27, 2018.

[4] *Joint Statement of the Fourth Round of the Six-Party Talks Beijing*, September 19, 2005, https://2001-2009.state.gov/r/pa/prs/ps/2005/53490.htm.

more likely that negotiations will end in disappointment and recrimination. Pyongyang may believe that the "complete denuclearization of the Korean peninsula" entails the United States withdrawing its extended deterrent commitment to the ROK, or even to end the U.S.-ROK Alliance. Indeed, Secretary Pompeo's statement that "complete" includes verification strongly suggests that establishing a common understanding of the terms being used will be an essential step in the diplomatic process.

Implications

- **Despite the president's claims, North Korea remains a significant threat to the United States and our allies in East Asia.** While the President's summit with Kim may have generated some goodwill and even built personal trust between the two leaders, North Korea has not given up a single warhead or ballistic missile. Its WMD production facilities are free to continue to manufacture their illegal arms, and not a single long-range artillery tube has been withdrawn from threatening the Seoul metropolitan area. North Korea has the same ability today to strike our allies, and possibly the United States, with nuclear weapons as it had before the President met Kim in Singapore.

- **The summit was a tremendous propaganda victory for Kim Jong Un.** This is why previous presidents have refused to meet with North Korean leaders – doing so in itself is a major concession and conveys tremendous legitimacy to the North Koreans. Images of Kim's meeting with the President of the United States will likely be used for years to show his people that he is respected and admired around the world and is considered an equal to the world's most powerful leaders. He can show the North Korean flag sitting next to the American flag and tell his people that his leadership has made the DPRK respected as an equal to the United States and recognized as a *de facto* nuclear power. And he can show the President saluting a North Korean General and tell his people that even the American President respects the Korean People's Army.

- **The Singapore summit injected new turbulence into U.S. alliances with Japan and the ROK.** The President's effusive praise of Kim Jong Un, and his willingness to meet with Kim and make significant concessions - despite making so little progress on denuclearization - inflamed allied concerns about the reliability of the United States. Tokyo has been more open about expressing their concerns, though it has been sure to praise the Trump administration for raising the issue of Japanese abductees with Kim[5] and its pledge to sustain economic sanctions until concrete steps toward denuclearization have been taken. In Seoul, the Moon administration has been officially supportive of the summit's outcomes and endorsed the president's decision to suspend military exercises.[6] Yet both Seoul and Tokyo are concerned about the suspension of exercises without corresponding North Korean concessions and without prior consultation. Such actions can, over time, damage the confidence of our allies in American reliability. Moreover, giving away significant mechanisms of alliance cooperation without coordination inflames fears that the United States will make another deal with North Korea that undermines their interests.

- **China got everything it wanted.** China has long sought for the United States to be committed to a diplomatic process and to suspend its military exercises in Korea. Beijing increasingly views issues on the Korean peninsula through the lens of geopolitical competition with the United States and seeks to diminish American power and influence in Korea. Further, China has long sought to cancel major U.S.-ROK joint military exercises and inject turbulence into the Alliance – both of which President Trump fulfilled unilaterally.

  Going forward, the Trump administration may have an opportunity to point to its tacit adoption of China's preferred strategy in order to sustain Beijing's continued enforcement of sanctions. This may be important, as China had already begun to soften its enforcement of sanctions weeks before the summit.

Next Steps

While it is too soon to know whether the diplomatic process that has been put in place will ultimately be successful, the United States has an opportunity to add specifics to the broad principles agreed to in Singapore. When looking forward to future engagements with North Korea, I want to make four concluding points.

- **Time is not on our side.** As Mike Pompeo stated as CIA Director in January of this year, North Korea was just "a handful of months away" from having the ability to

---

[5] "Japan PM Shinzo Abe thanks Donald Trump for raising North Korea's abductions with Kim Jong-un," *South China Morning Post,* June 12, 2018, http://www.scmp.com/news/asia/diplomacy/article/2150426/japan-pm-shinzo-abe-thanks-donald-trump-raising-north-koreas.

[6] Chang May Choon, "Trump-Kim summit: Jubilant Moon Jae In pledges to write 'new history' with North Korea," *The Straits Times,* June 12, 2018, https://www.straitstimes.com/asia/east-asia/trump-kim-summit-sleepless-skorea-president-moon-jae-in-hopes-for-new-era-of-complete.

strike the United States with nuclear weapons[7] – something the president and several of his predecessors have stated would be intolerable. Yet as Secretary of State following the Singapore summit, Pompeo stated that he expects there to be significant progress toward denuclearization by the end of 2020.

While North Korea has frozen its nuclear and ballistic missile testing, its ability to continue to mass-produce nuclear warheads and ballistic missiles – which Kim called for during his New Year's speech in January of this year – remains unrestrained. There is a danger that the United States has entered into an open-ended diplomatic process which would North Korea at a distinct advantage. While Secretary of State Pompeo's statement that he hopes to achieve North Korea's denuclearization by the end of 2020[8] suggests that he is aware of these time pressures, the fact that North Korea has not agreed to such a timeline suggests that this remains an unresolved issue.

As negotiations commence, North Korea will be able to continue to mass produce nuclear weapons and ballistic missiles unless we achieve a complete freeze of those programs. **One way for the United States to address time pressures on this negotiation would be to achieve a complete freeze of North Korea's nuclear and ballistic missile programs as an early step in a diplomatic process.**

- Another critical step in the denuclearization process will be to receive a full declaration from North Korea of its nuclear and chemical weapons programs, and the biological program it is suspected of possessing. Without such a declaration, it will be impossible to achieve denuclearization to any degree of confidence.

- To supplement the president's trust of Kim Jong Un trust, the United States could insist on strict inspection and verification regimes to accompany any concession North Korea may make toward denuclearization. Without verification, any North Korean concession should be viewed with deep skepticism.

- While I take the president at his word that human rights issues were discussed in Singapore, it is clear that these issues took a back seat. While I support the

---

[7] John Haltiwanger, "North Korea 'Handful of Months' From Being Able to Hit U.S. With Nuclear Weapon, CIA Director Warns," *Newsweek,* January 22, 2018, http://www.newsweek.com/north-korea-handful-months-being-able-hit-us-nuclear-weapon-cia-director-warns-786706.

[8] John Bowden, "Pompeo 'hopeful' North Korea will move toward denuclearization in Trump's first term," *The Hill,* June 13, 2018, http://thehill.com/policy/international/392059-pompeo-us-wants-concrete-steps-towards-north-korea-denuclearization.

administration's focus on denuclearization as its top priority with North Korea, a failure to keep international attention on these issues could result in a bad deal for the North Korean people. I find it difficult to imagine North Korea being accepted into the international community if it leaves its serious human rights issues unaddressed – even if North Korea were to genuinely denuclearize.

- **The United States should prepare for increased friction with China over maintaining pressure on North Korea.** I expect China will soften its enforcement of economic sanctions on North Korea, both to thwart U.S. efforts to maintain pressure on Pyongyang and to build a stronger bilateral relationship with Kim. The United States should be prepared to hold China accountable for its continued support of North Korea, even to the point of enacting secondary sanctions on Chinese entities that continue to do business with North Korea.

- **Considering the continuing threat posed by North Korea, the United States should ensure that its military forces and alliances in the region remain ready and robust.** This may entail tailoring what exercises remain so as to maintain necessary levels of force readiness and conducting genuine coordination efforts with our allies before a decision is made. Any strategy toward North Korea – be it diplomatic of military – is far stronger if allies are consulted and if the full weight of the United States and our allies can be brought to bear on a particular issue. Our allies are the foundation of American power in the Asia-Pacific and make significant contributions to the stability and prosperity of the region and to U.S. interests around the world. They deserve to be respected and consulted.

  Further, the people of the U.S. military make incredible sacrifices to defend the security and freedom of their fellow countrymen and our allies. During my time in the Department of Defense, I witnessed the incredible capabilities of the U.S. military and those of our allies. They deserve the resources needed to do their job effectively, and the ability to exercise as needed. Readiness saves lives, and ensures that our military remains the most awesome, feared fighting force in the history of the world. While negotiations with North Korea are certainly important as well, they do not have to come at the expense of the readiness of our forces or the security of our allies.

Going forward, we must remain clear-eyed about who we are dealing with. The threat from North Korea remains real, and Kim is not to be trusted. A credible, high-quality deal will be difficult to achieve, and even more difficult to implement and verify. After the pageantry of Singapore, the difficult work of diplomacy and denuclearization still lies ahead.

North Korean Denuclearization Commitments (1985-2018)

Description	Date	Commitment
NPT Signing	Dec 12, 1985	North Korea acceded to the very detailed nuclear Nonproliferation Treaty (NPT), but makes its membership contingent on the U.S. withdrawing nuclear weapons from the ROK.
South-North Joint Declaration	Jan 20, 1992	Agreed to not "test, manufacture, produce, receive, possess, store, deploy or use nuclear weapons" or "possess nuclear reprocessing and uranium enrichment facilities." North Korea also agreed to inspections for verification.
Joint Statement of the DPRK and the U.S.	June 11, 1993	Both sides endorsed the 1992 South-North Joint Declaration and agreed to the principles of "assurances against the threat and use of force, including nuclear weapons;" and "peace and security in a nuclear-free Korean Peninsula, including impartial application of full-scope safeguards."
Agreed Framework	Oct 21, 1994	North Korea committed to "freeze its graphite-moderated reactors and related facilities and will eventually dismantle these reactors and related facilities" agreed that the IAEA "will be allowed to monitor this freeze, and the DPRK will provide full cooperation to the IAEA for this purpose." North Korea also agreed to allow 8,000 spent nuclear reactor fuel elements to be removed to a third country. North Korea also agreed to remain in the NPT and allow implementation of its safeguards agreement under the Treaty.
U.S.-DPRK Joint Communique	Oct 12, 2000	Endorsed the Agreed Framework and strongly affirmed its role in achieving a nuclear weapons-free Korean Peninsula.
Withdrawal of the NPT	Jan 10, 2003	"Though we pull out of the NPT, we have no intention to produce nuclear weapons and our nuclear activities at this stage will be confined only to peaceful purposes such as the production of electricity"
Fourth Round of the Six-Party Talks Joint Statement	Sept 19, 2005	Reaffirmed that the goal of the Six-Party Talks is the verifiable denuclearization of the Korean Peninsula in a peaceful manner. Committed to abandoning all nuclear weapons and existing nuclear programs and returning, at an early date, to the Treaty on the Nonproliferation of Nuclear Weapons and to IAEA safeguards.
Joint Statement Following Six-Party Talks	Feb 13, 2007	North Korea agreed to shut down and seal for the purpose of eventual abandonment the Yonghyon nuclear facility, including the reprocessing facility, and invite back IAEA personnel to conduct all necessary monitoring and verifications as agreed between IAEA and the DPRK. North Korea also committed to discussing a list of all its nuclear programs as described in the Joint Statement, including plutonium extracted from used fuel rods, that would be abandoned pursuant to the Joint Statement.
Six-Party Talks, Second Phase for the Implementation of the 2005 Joint Statement	Oct 3, 2007	North Korea agreed to disable all existing nuclear facilities subject to abandonment under the September 2005 Joint Statement and the February 13 agreement. It also committed to disabling the 5-megawatt Experimental Reactor, the Reprocessing Plant, and the Nuclear Fuel Rod Fabrication Facility at Yongbyon by 31 December 2007. Pyongyang also agreed to provide a complete and correct declaration of all its nuclear programs, and reaffirmed its commitment not to transfer nuclear materials, technology, or know-how.
Second Inter-Korean Summit	Oct 4, 2007	The South and the North have agreed to work together to implement smoothly the September 19, 2005 Joint Statement and the February 13, 2007 Agreement achieved at the Six-Party Talks.
Leap Day Agreement	Feb. 29, 2012	North Korea announced it would suspend nuclear weapons tests and uranium enrichment, halt test launchings of long-range missiles, and allow international inspectors to monitor activities at its main nuclear complex.
Panmunjom Declaration	April 27, 2018	"South and North Korea confirmed the common goal of realizing, through complete denuclearization, a nuclear-free Korean Peninsula"
Singapore Summit Joint Statement	June 12, 2018	"Reaffirming the April 27, 2018 Panmunjom Declaration, the DPRK commits to work toward complete denuclearization of the Korean Peninsula."

Mr. YOHO. Thanks, everyone, for your testimony. I look forward to getting into the questions.

You know, you brought up—Mr. Denmark, you brought up a very good point. It's a tremendous propaganda win for Mr. Kim and I think most of the world sees that and I think a lot of people here feel that, too.

But it's also a tremendous opportunity. I was born in 1955. That conflict has been going on ever since then. You know, we are operating under an armistice for all those years.

It's time to bring finality to something, and when we get to that point then you have certainty, and when you have certainty you can develop trade and all those things in the economy.

And until we get to that point, we are not going to have that kind of stability on that peninsula, as I think we all agree.

What I see with what President Trump has done is he's changed the dynamics of negotiation, and, you know, whether it's good or bad, the future will tell us.

But what I see he has given the ball or a pass to Mr. Kim, and it's an opportunity. What he does with it will determine the next steps.

You know, some people look at it as a rope—if he does bad that he'll hang himself with it. Others will see, you know what, this is a chance that they can change the dynamics on North Korea—of North Korea and develop an economic engine, and I can only think, because we were talking about when he was in Singapore.

Here you have a young leader of a country that doesn't have much outside exposure. Thirty-four years old—goes and sees Xi Jinping in China, sees their economic engine there. Goes to Singapore, sees the economic engine.

The things that he sees, he has to go home thinking why can't this be my country. Now he's got to deal with how do I bring this in there. Hopefully, that's what he's seeing, and I think with the President allowing him—and I don't want to use the word legitimacy—but allowing him to move into the negotiations, I think this is, as we've said multiple times, historic.

Where it goes from here will be based on the next steps, and it's going to be a step by step process, and I think you have all brought up a very good point that we have to make sure that the sanctions stay ratcheted up and so I think along those lines, as we start negotiation, what I see as one of the most important things is the definitions—definitions of denuclearization—what does that mean to the North and what does that mean to the peninsula and the rest of the world.

Verification—and I want to ask the question, who should do the verification? Should we rely on the IAEA that I, personally, don't have a lot of confidence in, or should it be a coalition of the partner countries—South Korea, North Korea, us, and maybe for balancing, allow somebody from China or Russia there?

I would like to have your opinion on that and then we'll ask you a few more questions. Bruce?

Mr. KLINGNER. Verification is an issue dear to my heart. I was a chief of the arms control staff at CIA and I served on one of the negotiating delegations overseas.

So it's really a two-part thing. One is the measures that you have in the treaty, in which everyone knows exactly what their responsibilities are and you provide the details of how that is done.

And then that's used in conjunction with your national technical means so that you can verify that. But you do need on-site inspection.

So with the inspectors, whether it's IAEA or a coalition or whether we call it other things, I think what you will need to do is have on any teams at least one American and one Chinese representative, because the Americans are going to want to have eyes on where we see if something is a violation or not, and if we call it a violation China would likely disagree. So you probably need them there on the same team.

Mr. YOHO. Right.

Mr. KLINGNER. Now, things—when you get to actual fissile material and actual nuclear weapons, you would probably want to restrain that to the five members of the P-5 who have nuclear weapons.

So if you're getting into that level of radioactive and nuclear weapons, I think you keep it to a very select few countries.

Mr. YOHO. Okay.

Mr. KLINGNER. But the U.S. wouldn't have enough inspectors to man all of the inspections. So you would need other countries. But I think we'd have to have U.S. representation on every team.

Mr. YOHO. All right.

Let me go down to Dr. Green.

Mr. GREEN. We, in the Six-Party Talks, did considerable work on this with other nuclear weapon states, principally Britain and France, but also Russia, which was helpful at the time, and to a lesser extent, China, which has very limited experience in arms control.

The work has been done on what this should look like and the State Department and the CIA and others would have it.

As Bruce points out, the IAEA has a role in safeguards in places like Yongbyon, but nuclear weapons they don't do, so that would require some accommodation of the permanent five and most likely U.S. and Russia, Britain, and France would be at the core of it.

As Bruce points out, China has a major equity, and although they have less experience, should probably be there.

Stanford University did a study that suggested even under a permissive environment, in the very unlikely event that Kim Jong-un really wants to denuclearize, this is a 10- to 15-year process.

And even then, the scientists and engineers have all that information in their heads and what do you do with them? So the reality is there is no end date for CVID. It's a constant ongoing process.

The other problem is precisely because it has to be in iterations that North Koreans and China will use that to try to get rewards for small increments and to hold up progress.

So one of the tough challenges for the Secretary of State is what's an early harvest that shows us seriousness. I think a declaration is one of them. Getting out fissile material weapons might be next.

Mr. YOHO. All right. Mr. Denmark—20 seconds.

Mr. DENMARK. I don't have much. I thought the answers were very good. I agree that the IAEA has an important role to play.

But there is a difference between inspection, verification, and actually pulling the weapons out—that the P-5 is going to have an important role to play.

The different countries have various levels of capability. I am especially concerned about China's ability to actually handle those responsibly.

But overall, I think it's important to make sure that any verification regime is robust. As Dr. Green said, this is going to require very intense—very intrusive inspections. That's difficult for any country to really accept and for a country as self-isolated as North Korea it's very difficult to see.

But it's going to be an extremely long process. There is really no such thing a quick denuclearization.

Mr. YOHO. Right. Thank you.

I will next turn to the ranking member, Mr. Sherman of California.

Mr. SHERMAN. Thank you. One bit of disagreement with Dr. Green. It may take 10, 15 years to root out every piece of the North Korea nuclear program.

But if they stop the centrifuges, dismantle them, ship fissile material, that is something Iran did in 90 days and could have done quicker, and that would make us all sleep a little better.

I do have a comment or two about Mr. Rohrabacher's opening statement. First is I believe it's President Eisenhower who is the President who did the most to bring peace to the Korean Peninsula.

And second, I want President Trump to succeed and, beyond that, I have defined success with a lower, more achievable standard not only that any Democrat in the room but any Republican in the room, although we haven't heard from the gentlelady from Hawaii yet, but in a much more achievable lower standard for success than anyone else I know actively involved in foreign policy.

But as Mr. Green points out, just doing a meeting that's not an achievement. That's a concession. The last four or five Presidents were all begged by North Korea to do this meeting. They all decided it was a concession they were unwilling to make.

I want to focus a bit, because we have a Japan expert with us here—Dr. Green. It is very anomalous that you have in Japan the third largest economy in the world who, as of now, is doing nothing with its own military forces or preparing to do nothing with its military forces to defend its own back yard.

Now, the Japanese constitution talks about this or that, but the U.N.—the mission to defend North Korea is a United Nations mission, and many countries believe that meeting their U.N. obligations is something they're legally able to do.

What do we do to have the Japanese military be willing and prepared to be part of the effort to defend South Korea?

I realize that not all the problems are in Tokyo.

Mr. GREEN. No, they're enough. First of all, I think you put that very well.

North Korea could, in a month, in a week, ship out centrifuges, fissile material, nuclear weapons, and in a month or 2 ship out all of it.

The full CVID is what's going to take 10 or 15 years. So I think—I agree with you actually. I think that's an important point for the record.

Under Prime Minister Abe, Japan has revised the interpretation of the constitution to allow for the first time in the post-war period Japanese forces to plan jointly with the U.S. to move and operate together, and that's a significant move.

He's moved—he's increased the defense budget a little bit. Japan should spend more. He's moving—he said he's going to buy new weapons systems that Japan had never had.

Mr. SHERMAN. But how do we get those joint trilateral exercises?

Mr. GREEN. So that is a problem. The Japanese defense forces are keen to exercise with Korea. The Korean defense forces are keen to exercise with Japan because they recognize what you said. If we are not working together it's dangerous for all of us.

It's the political level that's the problem. Right now the——

Mr. SHERMAN. Is it politically dangerous for a South Korean President to say hey, we are going to have joint trilateral exercises? Would that have been dangerous before Singapore? Is it dangerous after Singapore—politically dangerous?

Mr. GREEN. I don't think it is. It's not easy, but I don't think it's difficult and, frankly, if we pushed——

Mr. SHERMAN. And how difficult would it be for Abe to——

Mr. GREEN. Abe would do it. The problem is that the South Korean side, as Bruce and Abe know well, the South Korean side is not satisfied with the agreement that Prime Minister Abe made with the previous President about historical issues like the comfort women, and that's a political and social and other problem.

But in terms of the militaries—Japanese and Korean realize they have to work together jointly and, you know, in my view, the administration should be pushing harder on this.

The exercises we do with the South Koreans are suspended. The South Korean military is going to go ahead with another exercise to defend the small island of Dokdo against the Japanese. That's the wrong enemy.

Mr. SHERMAN. What?

Mr. GREEN. The wrong enemy, yes.

So I am glad you flagged it in your opening comments. I think it should be a priority. I think that the—that the Japanese and Korean military experts, diplomats, should think about the North Korean problem, recognize it. It's the politicians who have to be pushed to increase the collaboration between the two.

Mr. SHERMAN. Thank you.

Mr. YOHO. Next we'll go to Dana Rohrabacher from California.

Mr. ROHRABACHER. A couple of thoughts. I am sorry I would disagree with my colleague and the witness as well. You both seem to be underestimating the antagonism of the Korean people to the Japanese.

And I am sorry, it's not a good thing. I don't like it. But it better be a factor in how we create a more peaceful situation in that part of the world.

The Koreans have never forgiven the Japanese for the Second World War, and but that does not mean we should not—we should not be moving forward with a plan that would increase Japan's at least capacity in that region but not necessarily having military maneuvers aimed at something going on in Korea. I think that would be counterproductive.

With that said, let me also note when I said that this whole thing is a, you know, deja vu all over again. Let us note that of my colleagues who are saying we didn't accomplish anything and my witnesses suggest it wasn't accomplished, that Reagan, when he was negotiating, when he went to Reykjavik and elsewhere, this was predicated how we ended up turning what was a slamming of the door—Reykjavik—to another situation was Ronald Reagan proposed the zero option, and he was—by the way, most people forget that.

And, again, castigated by the liberal Democrat opponents of Ronald Reagan as being a fraud and you're never going to get them to agree to that.

We want the nuclear freeze, which would have frozen the Soviets into a—into a superior position with nuclear weapons and Reagan said no, we are going to go for the zero option and he was called— they said he's being disingenuous. The Democratic attacks on Trump are almost exactly the same, and the fact is that in the end the Soviets agreed to the zero option, and in the end we eliminated a whole schedule of nuclear weapons in Europe because yes, the President did not demand immediately to have something to show for every meeting that he was in and had a long strategy that worked.

I believe that's what's going on right now, and our President has opened the door. He's opened the door, and I agree with Mr. Kinzinger, I should say—not Kissinger—who pointed out military— maintaining a strong military possibility and that's why I was talking about Japan and helping them build forces there, was an important component about bringing together the end of the Cold War and would be important to hear as well.

In the Cold War, while Ronald Reagan had his hand out, he also was supporting mujahadeen guerillas in Afghanistan, the contras in Nicaragua, various elements in eastern Europe who we were supporting under cover like Walesa and others. And so my colleague is exactly right, it needs to be a two-fisted thing.

But I have no reason—I do not believe there is any reason for us to suspect that this President—we keep treating him as if he doesn't know what he's doing. He understands the basics, and there's a fellow who wrote a book in my district called "No Profit Without Risk." His name is Bob Mayer. Bob Mayer is a very successful businessman.

Our President is very successful businessman. He realizes there will be not progress without some risk, and what you—and what— but you should not castigate this President and undermine his position as being taking—as possibly having a rational approach rather than just dismissing him as oh, this is just so risky—we shouldn't be doing this.

I think he's putting us in a position, like Reagan did when he said the zero option, not nuclear freeze, to actually put us in a position to end the conflict on the Korean Peninsula.

And the goal isn't just taking nuclear weapons out of the hands of North Korea. The goal is to unify Korea in the end under a somewhat democratic country.

And one last note, and I want your comments on this—sorry I am taking up all this time—but the fact is that this Kim is different than his father and his father's father.

And when you say that, as my colleague just said, but he went to Singapore, maybe he saw the potential of the West—this man, this young leader Kim, he was educated in Switzerland at an elite and prestigious school.

He knows so much more than what his father and his father's father knew that perhaps these things that we are talking about make sense that you're dealing with a rational person rather than a rabid Marxist dog like his dad and his grandfather.

So I am sorry. I've used up my time. Could they have a minute to comment on—feel free to disagree.

Mr. YOHO. Real briefly, if you can comment.

Mr. KLINGNER. I think in many ways Kim Jong-un is different from his predecessors but in many ways he is similar. It perhaps is a more effective implementation of a three generation game plan by the North Koreans.

North Korea has had a two-page play book of alternating threats, attacks with charm offensives, although with North Korea it tends to be more offensive than charming.

With Kim Jong-un, he, for 6 years, only did the first page of his father's play book and he did it on steroids with an accelerated test schedule.

And since January he switched to the second page and also done that sort of on steroids, where he's now had the revolving door of summits.

So the whiplash effect is strong in going from one extreme to the other. But I think it's still trying to implement the objectives of his father and his grandfather of being accepted as a nuclear state, of reducing the pressure and isolation on North Korea, getting economic benefits but on North Korean terms.

They want to get the economic benefits but they don't want to open their country to what they see as the contagion of outside influence.

Mr. YOHO. Okay. Thank you.

We are going to go on, just out of respect for the other members.

Mr. Connolly from Virginia.

Mr. CONNOLLY. Thank you, Mr. Chairman, and let me thank you for putting together an intellectually honest panel. I've gone to way too many committee hearings on this committee over the years where we have a skewed panel. Even the title of the hearing predetermines the outcome of the hearing.

Mr. YOHO. We try to be fair and balanced.

Mr. CONNOLLY. Well, you have been more than that.

No, seriously, I really thank you because I think we are having an intellectually honest conversation about something that's terribly important.

My friend from California I think does not accurately recall history, even though he worked for Ronald Reagan. My recollection of the Reykjavik summit was that when Ronald Reagan said, why don't we just get rid of all nuclear weapons, it was the neocons in his own administration who were shocked and distressed, not liberal Democrats.

And secondly, I must remind my friend from California, I sat here for 8 long years and I don't remember my friends on the other side of the aisle giving the very kind of consideration he now asks of this President to President Obama. And what's sauce for the goose is sauce for the gander.

So we Democrats reserve our right, the right you exercised for 8 years, to criticise this President and we are going to do it carefully but with some zeal.

Let me—let me summarize, if I may, what I've heard from all three of our witnesses. We have a history of violations by the North. Don't get too excited about anything they sign on to.

Added to the fact that this joint statement after the so-called summit actually lacked specificity. I think it was you, Mr. Klingner, who said—or maybe you, Dr. Green—it actually is less meat on the table in this statement than some of the previous ones.

We still have a huge human rights problem. Again, I was listening to my friend from California. You would never guess—you know, he had his uncle executed in a horrifying way. You'd never guess he still presides over gulags of tens of thousands of North Koreans. You'd never guess that he had his step-brother assassinated—killed at a modern airport in Asia, but okay.

You have the effect—I think, Dr. Green, you talked about the de facto lessening of sanctions with China. This kind of gives a little bit of a green light to China, maybe not others about certainly China, and that's not a good thing, given the fact that most of their trade is with China.

We have the recognition of their nuclear status de facto by having the summit by the United States. WE elevate his stature, which they've been seeking, as you pointed out, Dr. Green, for the previous three or four administrations. This is the first one to give it to him.

And in return, we've gotten no commitment on denuclearization, no commitment on inspections, no commitment on metrics, and as I said in my statement, the problem President Trump has is by ripping up Iran, which was working and that had very specific metrics, one has to presume, since he decided that was inadequate, that with respect to North Korea or any nuclear threshold state, we are going to have higher metrics—we are going to have a higher standard they have to meet. And I don't know how you do that, frankly, with North Korea. I think Iran complicates the problem.

But I also think just this so-called summit—I don't want to take anything away from shaking hand and having a photo op, but I think there's danger in terms of the expectations that have been raised, in the concessions de facto that have been granted.

I now welcome you to comment on that.

Doctor—Mr. Klingner.

Mr. KLINGNER. I've been working on North Korea for 25 years so I tend to be skeptical and cynical. But perhaps you are even more skeptical than I.

No, I agree. I would say the summit as—it's a first step. We can discuss, debate how successful it was, how good a first step it is.

But as you know, my colleagues and I have tried to identify the things that we need to do to put the meat on the bones and——

Mr. CONNOLLY. Yes, but I am not trying to be skeptical. I am trying to raise—I am trying to be realistic, and what I listed was actually feeding back what I heard from your testimony, which I thought was very helpful.

You know, yes, be hopeful but let's be realistic. Not like we don't have a history here.

Mr. KLINGNER. Right. No, exactly, and just to boil it down I would say is we need very detailed texts and then very good verification.

You know, not only do they have a different definition of denuclearization, but when they define the Korean Peninsula, it's anything that influences the peninsula, including our bombers in Guam and our submarines and our aircraft carriers.

So we need to get the terms straight and we need to look at sort of the arms control treaties we had to be very, very specific—a very detailed contract with someone who has cheated us many times in the past.

Mr. CONNOLLY. If the chair would allow the other two witnesses to answer and then I yield back my time.

Mr. YOHO. Go ahead.

Mr. CONNOLLY. I thank the chair.

Mr. GREEN. So, Representative Connolly, I think you have accurately captured the core points we are all trying to make and that, I think, points to the important oversight role Congress should have in this and in any negotiation the negotiators help by a good cop-bad cop, and there's a role that could be a bipartisan role for this committee and for the Congress, in my view.

If I could very briefly pick up on Mr. Rohrabacher's point about Ronald Reagan. You know, it was Richard Nixon, a conservative Republican, who changed relations with China. There is an argument that we should not dismiss, that any conservative Republican President can do this because of the curious politics of it all.

However, I think there are two lessons from Reagan that would be important to remember.

You know Ronald Reagan went to Reykjavik, having presented an absolutely unwavering commitment to human rights and democratic values, and a clear and unchanged, unrivalled, frankly, commitment to our allies.

When the Soviets deployed SS-20s in Europe and NATO, he went right back, toe to toe, with tactical nuclear weapons. If we look for the opportunity for a Republican President to do something like this with North Korea, it is absolutely essential for President Trump to remember what Ronald Reagan did.

And what we've heard so far has not been a Reagan-like commitment to democratic values, to human rights, and to our allies, which is an essential backstop precisely because North Korea is targeting the U.S.-Korea alliance as the center of gravity they don't want to break and China is targeting our alliances as a whole, and that's an important—the Reagan parallel could work. But I think those two caveats are absolutely essential to remember.

Mr. YOHO. Mr. Denmark, real quick.

Mr. DENMARK. Yes, sir. I agree that you summarized the points that we've been making a great deal, and I think—I agree that there's a tremendous role that the Congress has in terms of oversight.

The one point I would like to add and it feeds into some of the discussion that was had earlier but I didn't have time to in my opening statement, one of the key aspects of any negotiation is to know what the other guy on the other side of the table wants—what they're trying to get out of this negotiation.

And if you look at everything that Kim Jong-un has done—you said earlier that Kim Jong-un may be different from his father or his grandfather—since taking power, Kim Jong-un accelerated nuclear testing, accelerated ballistic missile testing.

If you look at his New Year's statement from January of this year, his version of the State of the Union Address, he embraced nuclear weapons, declared the whole program a success and said that he wanted to turn toward economic development, but as a nuclear power.

I have yet to see any indication that Kim Jong-un is looking at disarmament or denuclearization. My sense is that he believes he wants to be entering into arms controls negotiations the way that we were doing in Reykjavik, not denuclearization negotiations, and if you have a good sense of right, I strongly recommend that you would read the New Year's address.

The translation is in English. It's very clear. He's looking to engage the world as a nuclear power, and until we have a good understanding of what he's actually trying to get out of it, these negotiations are going to be difficult to even move a bit forward because we have different objections in mind.

Mr. YOHO. Thank you.

Next we'll go to Ambassador and Congresswoman Ann Wagner from Missouri.

Mrs. WAGNER. Thank you, Mr. Chairman.

The U.S. faces two threats in Northeast Asia—North Korea and China. My father served in the Korean War and the stalemate in the region persists to this day.

America's intervention in Korea in 1950 was a strategic success in preventing an important buffer region from becoming a zone of communist influence and strengthening the United States' hand in the broader Cold War. Cold War is over, but today the North still serves as a buffer state for China.

Rapprochement between the U.S. and North Korea could possibly threaten China's influence over the Kim regime.

Dr. Green, North Korea is useful to China because it distracts and challenges the U.S. and our South Korean alliance.

At the same time, the Kim regime is vulnerable because of its strategic and economic dependency on China. China is North Korea's real long-term threat, not the United States.

Do you believe China has an interest, Dr. Green, in our negotiations failing?

Mr. GREEN. You know, I think we don't get to read about the Chinese debate because they don't have an open vibrant political system like we do.

But I think in Beijing they are as confounded by North Korea as we are, in many respects. I think you accurately captured their strategic view but there are huge debates within the leadership compound in Zhongnanhai, I am sure.

I think from China's perspective, the operative approach is not today—don't let North Korea collapse today—don't have unification today—kick this can down the road.

In 10 years, in 20 years, in 30 years China will be more powerful. It will have more control over North and South Korea. China will be in a position to affect unification of a peninsula with no American alliance.

So China has every incentive to lower tensions but also to just kick this can down the road, and that's our problem, and part of the solution is our alliances, because China assumes it will be more powerful and have more influence over South Korea as time passes.

But if we are faithful to our allies, if we are strong on trilateral defense cooperation with Japan and Korea, if we don't say we want to get out of Korea, if we do all of those things, we signal to China that North Korea is making our alliances stronger—thank you very much, Beijing—so if you are worried about that, you need to put more pressure on your friends in Pyongyang—the game of alliances and U.S. and China is an essential part of how we get purchase on the——

Mrs. WAGNER. How can the U.S. best manage China's interests as it negotiates with Kim? Because, frankly, kicking the can down the road is a negotiation failure at this point in time.

Mr. GREEN. Yes, in the sense that we won't get a result. It's a success for China and interests converge in North Korea because it just sort of prevents the U.S. from taking action.

Look, we had the Six-Party Talks. They failed to get North Korea to denuclearize. I was involved in that at the time. One useful thing about it was it got China, Russia, Japan, Korea all around the table. They all have equities. Only China, North Korea, U.S., and South Korea would be in a peace negotiation to replace armistice.

We will need a broader diplomatic framework that gets——

Mrs. WAGNER. I am running out of time.

Mr. Klingner, is it possible to check the growth of Chinese power through our negotiations with Kim? Namely, what could we do to turn the North into a buffer zone for our own interests?

Mr. KLINGNER. Well, I think the North Korean-Chinese relationship is strained. It's more strained now than under the previous leaders in North Korea.

You know, 5,000 years of history and 1,000 invasions or so have caused North Korea to have a very suspicious view of its neighbors. They see it as a shrimp amongst whales.

Each of the leaders in North Korea has warned that China is a bigger threat to North Korea than the U.S. because of its intent to influence North Korea.

So the North Korean nuclear program was a response to feeling that both the Soviet Union and China were not going to protect North Korea to the degree that they needed.

So I think North Korea is playing all these countries, all these neighbors, off against each other. The thing with the alliances is that they are multi-purpose tool, so that they are not only deterring and defending against the North Korean threat but they're also serving to protect not only U.S. and allied interests——

Mrs. WAGNER. Thank you. I hate to interrupt.

But Mr. Denmark, we know Kim has been talking with Xi Jinping throughout this process. China has lost influence in North Korea's top circles of power. But what role is Xi playing in our negotiations? Do you think China has the ability to influence Kim as he enters negotiations with the U.S., and how?

Mr. DENMARK. I do believe that Xi Jinping has a multiplying effect. I think his primary message from all these meetings that he's been having with Kim Jong-un is to show that China has a critical role to play and China will not be bypassed.

The most important role that China will have in these negotiations will be in maintaining economic pressure. As the Trump administration has said, they want to make sure that North Korea remains under significant economic pressure until it makes significant steps toward denuclearization.

The challenge, of course, is that the vast majority of international trade for North Korea goes through China, and China has, in the past, proven inconsistent, you can say, in its willingness to engage those sanctions and to enforce those sanctions.

One of the challenges that we are going to have, going forward, is that many in China, as Dr. Green mentioned, many in China increasingly see dynamics on the Korean Peninsula through the lens of geopolitical competition with the United States.

And if China sees progress in some area as being—sees increased sanctions, for example, as being an American interest, that may be one reason why China may be less willing to enforce some of those sanctions, because they see it potentially as helping the United States.

Mrs. WAGNER. Thank you.

My time has expired. I appreciate the chair's indulgence. I yield back.

Mr. YOHO. Thank you.

Next we'll go to Ms. Tulsi Gabbard from Hawaii.

Ms. GABBARD. Thank you, Mr. Chairman. I thank the gentlemen for being here and sharing your insights.

I think there's been a lot of focus on the geopolitical considerations and impacts of these negotiations. But very little focus on the seriousness of the North Korea nuclear threat on the United States.

As the chairman mentioned, I represent Hawaii. Being in the middle of the Pacific this is something that is an ever present concern for our residents and people who live in our State.

The false missile alert that we had in January of this year brought things into light that many others really didn't consider.

So the seriousness of these talks and this diplomatic path failing, very high stakes, and why, I believe it's important that these talks happened. Important first step, as everyone has said, clearly lacking in critical details, lacking in written plan of execution on exactly how this will be done. North Korea is still a threat that is posed to us. But we all hope for success and want to be supportive in that.

I have a few questions. I am, first of all wondering what your thoughts are on should a nuclear agreement come out of these talks, what role approval by the House and Senate has, whether this should require ratification by the Senate or take a similar route as the previous Iran nuclear deal in allowing for congressional disapproval?

If we are talking about permanent denuclearization being most successful, what role do you see Congress playing in that?

Mr. KLINGNER. I believe that achieving many issues with North Korea, not only denuclearization but a potential peace treaty and normalization relations, are of such critical importance to the United States that it should be a matter for more than just the executive branch.

I think the legislative branch should be involved. So whether that's a formal treaty or interaction with the executive branch, I think it is of such importance, particularly a peace treaty and denuclearization.

Ms. GABBARD. So you don't see any major difference between ratification of the treaty by the Senate versus some other mechanism of approval or disapproval?

Mr. KLINGNER. I don't know enough about the mechanics of it— a Senate ratification versus other means.

Mr. GREEN. The President had waiver authority in the 18 or so pieces of legislation that Trading With the Enemy Act and so forth—terrorism—these sanctions give the President a Presidential waiver. So legally he can lift sanctions in the process of rewarding North Korea for steps toward denuclearization. But the President has talked about a peace regime—a peace declaration—a peace treaty that would have to be ratified by the Senate.

If the United States negotiates a normalization that has to be ratified, and if there is to be aid for North Korea, it would come through the Asia Development Bank, the World Bank, maybe China's Belt and Road. But Congress would have authorities and control of the budget.

So bottom line is if this does move forward there's going to be a major congressional role even if the President has national security waiver authority on sanctions, and one way to construct this would be, like, the Helsinki process in the Cold War with the Soviet Union to have a broad framework where there are baskets, such as economic development, human rights, conventional weapons, and confidence building nuclear weapons and with the aim of ultimately moving toward peace treaty ratification denuclearization and begin building that process with Congress through hearings and so forth to anticipate what Congress would expect.

I think maybe not in the next month or 2 but early on in the process that framework should be set up.

Ms. GABBARD. Dr. Green, you mentioned earlier, I think, about how CVID is an ongoing process. It's not something that really has a hard finish.

A lot has been—I think you all talked about the different types of verification measures that would be needed. Can you talk about the irreversible part of that acronym and how that can be executed, especially given your history in this?

Mr. GREEN. Well, we never got irreversible, ever, not in the Six-Party Talks.

Ms. GABBARD. Is it possible?

Mr. GREEN. If the North Koreans turn over fissile material, nuclear weapons, that's irreversible in the sense that they can't use those anymore.

But that doesn't stop them from continuing to spin centrifuges to make more uranium-based weapons if we don't know where all the facilities are.

So the only way to get irreversible really, aside from bits and pieces, is full inspections, and the North Koreans have not even let us look in the keyhole in the negotiations to date. The first step will be a declaration.

Ms. GABBARD. How do you deal with the nuclear scientists that they have?

Mr. GREEN. Well, you know, Senators Nunn and Lugar have legislation to do this with the Soviets that was—appears to have been pretty effective and I saw they both spoke recently and met with the President, I understand.

So that might be a model—the Nunn-Lugar legislation to employ scientists and engineers, and it's also one we suggested to the North Koreans in the Six-Party Talks as a way to help compensate them, basically, by hiring scientists and engineers for other projects.

Ms. GABBARD. Thank you.

Thank you, Mr. Chairman.

Mr. YOHO. Thank you.

Next we'll go to Ms. Dina Titus from Nevada.

Ms. TITUS. Well, thank you, Mr. Chairman, and I thank all of you for testimony. It's been most interesting.

I share in your skepticism about this so-called agreement and some of the vagueness of the terms—what's the time and what's the possible verification—what does denuclearization really mean.

Also, President Trump has been getting a lot of credit for putting us in a better position with Korea—than we've been in for a while.

But let us not forget that it was some of his saber rattling and his belligerent rhetoric that got us to the kind of a crisis situation—the fire and fury, as you recall. So I don't think we should give the arsonist too much credit for putting out the fire.

You were talking earlier about, you know, some of the tactics of diplomacy and I think language is a very big part of that and the language that you use.

Our President is not a master of the English language, much less any other one, and he doesn't stick to the script or read the teleprompter or take notes or believe in preparing.

One of the uses of language I thought that might hinder this diplomatic effort is when he used the same language as North Korea and China used about the joint military exercises and called them provocative. That's what they have been saying they are.

We have had other reasons for why those exercises took place but now just kind of on the spur of the moment he canceled them because they are provocative.

I wonder if, moving forward in these diplomatic relations, we aren't making a mistake using the same language that our adversaries use as opposed to making our own case.

Mr. Denmark, would you comment on that?

Mr. DENMARK. As I said earlier, ma'am, my sense is that these exercises are not provocative. They're defensive. They're stabilizing. They're legal, which is why I've always opposed the so-called freeze for freeze proposal that the Chinese made, and I am trying to equate some degree of equality between these two.

But I think, if you take a step back, referring to these exercises as provocative really has broader implications than just on the Korean Peninsula. It suggests that these exercises are done to provoke not just North Korea but potentially the exercises that we have all around the world can now be pointed to by our adversaries as provocative.

And so I think it has global implications in that way. But at the same time, my sense is that it raises the bar for if the President decides he wants to reinstate these exercises, wants to do any of these major exercises again in Korea, then it allows North Korea, it allows China to say, you said that these are provocative—you're only doing these to provoke us—it's not about readiness—it's not about deterrence—you said it's about provocation and this is exactly what you're trying to do.

So I think by using that language, I agree that languages is absolutely important in diplomacy. My concern is that by using this language it helps feed into the arguments that China and North Korea have been making for a long time.

Ms. TITUS. I agree.

You know, we've heard a lot about China and North Korea and Japan. There are other players in the area that are going to be affected by this that I think we need to take into account, too. You saw Mongolia wanted to host the summit, Singapore, you know, India. We need to look at other allies there as we move forward on this.

Also, I would ask you, I am inclined to think that North Korea is not going to give up their nuclear weapons because that's what got them to the table. That's what got the U.S. there, and now they want to play on that stage.

At what point in these negotiations, going forward, do we shift our focus from denuclearization to nuclear control or arms control?

Mr. KLINGNER. Well, going along with the theme of words matter, North Korea defines denuclearization as global arms control, and as my colleagues have said it is as a self-professed member of the nuclear club, North Korea will say, we'll go to zero when you go to zero.

So we need to move away from defining or allowing North Korea to define the denuclearization, which is a U.N. requirement, in North Korean terms of arms control.

So we need to keep focusing on what is required under numerous U.N. resolutions.

Mr. GREEN. I would not bet a lot of money that this is going to lead to CVID. If it goes well, then maybe in a year or 2 this committee will be debating the deal we have, and the deal we have is probably going to be if it's—best case scenario, in my view, North Korea freezes the Yongbyon plutonium facility or North Korea agrees to turn over certain facilities.

It's a piece of the program, and then the debate will be how much do we lift sanctions—do we normalize relations—do we give them economic aid.

And people can have a reasonable debate about that if we are lucky enough to get that far. My own bias would be reward them incrementally with humanitarian aid and other things but do not normalize or do other things that undermine the credibility of our commitment to allies.

WE should be always remembering, as I said, that there are two chess games going on. One is with North Korea but the other one is with China, and our critical advantage in both, but especially the one with China, is our alliances.

So let's not jeopardize our alliances for a partial deal. Let's pay something if we have to, but make sure that our alliances and our military readiness and deterrence are intact and, in fact, are getting stronger.

Mr. DENMARK. I believe that the United States should not drop its commitment to denuclearization. That said, I do think that positive progress is positive progress, and if we are able to make a partial deal that improves stability, that reduces the risk of war, that would be work to some degree of concessions, although I agree with Dr. Green that it is not worth giving everything for a partial deal.

My sense, as I've said before, is that North Korea thinks they're in the mode of arms control negotiations, not denuclearization negotiations.

And my fear for accepting a partial goal would that be the North Koreans would say okay, we got what we wanted—we are going to stop here.

So I think it's always important to maintain—keep things back that they need—that they want in order to continue to have pressure to move forward on negotiations. But, again, positive progress is positive progress.

Ms. TITUS. Thank you.

Thank you, Mr. Chairman.

Mr. YOHO. Next, if you guys can tolerate it, we'll go back. Not that it's bad, but a second round of questions and I am going to let the ranking member start because he's got to get to another meeting.

Mr. SHERMAN. First, as to—and I will pick up on the gentlelady from Hawaii's point—from a North Korean perspective, for them to settle for an agreement that is just with the executive branch would show that they're not paying attention.

Gaddafi gave up his incipient nuclear program in return for an agreement with the executive branch. We all know that Kim Jong-un does not want to follow the Libya model. And Iran reached an agreement with only the executive branch and then the next head of the executive branch abrogated it.

That may not be as important to Iran because they want a relationship with Europe more than they want a relationship with the
United States. But in North Korea's circumstance, it would deprive
them of very much of what they're negotiating for.

I would also point out that if we release half the sanctions and
we get half of what we need in terms of arms limitations rollbacks,
that's a much worse deal for us because if you give up half the
sanctions that's like you did have your foot on his neck and now
you lift it most of the way.

Well, that's bad for his people, because they won't enjoy prosperity. But it gives him enough economic clout to survive and to
make sure that the finest in European luxuries are bestowed upon
the top 3,000 or 4,000 families in the countries.

So he doesn't need all these sanctions released. He only needs
half of them released to assure everything he cares about.

I want to ask—and I don't know which of you is in addition to
being a foreign policy expert a strategic arms expert—but let's talk
first about testing—what do they need to test.

Have they reached the point where they've tested a thermonuclear hydrogen bomb or do they need to do more testing to feel
that they are capable of creating that?

Who has an answer? Mr. Denmark.

Mr. DENMARK. So I can give my sense. I think Bruce has some
thoughts as well.

We've seen them conduct tests. We don't get perfect sense of
what it is. What we saw is a large device.

Mr. SHERMAN. Right.

Mr. DENMARK. When it comes to testing I think the key thought
is that we should not apply our standards of testing to North
Korea. We have very high standards of testing for the reliability of
our missiles, of everything.

For North Korea, they just need to have the plausible capability.
They don't need to test it——

Mr. SHERMAN. So have they reached that plausible capability
with regard to thermonuclear weapons, even if they agree not to
test nuclear weapons in the future?

Mr. DENMARK. My judgment is that they're probably confident
enough in order to be able to do it.

Mr. SHERMAN. Does any—do either of our other panellists disagree?

Mr. GREEN. I agree the one technical hurdle they appear not to
have crossed is the ability for their weapon to reenter the atmos-
phere without burning up.

Mr. SHERMAN. Yes. That's the delivery system.

Mr. GREEN. But I think they——

Mr. SHERMAN. Now, on delivery systems, keep in mind they can
have a submarine in a small boat deliver one—not to Chicago but
to Los Angeles or Honolulu. I guess Las Vegas is safe from that.

Mr. GREEN. So they've achieved an acceptable level of ICBM capability.

Mr. SHERMAN. So they clearly have proven missile capacity with
regard to Tokyo and Seoul but they'd need a reentry vehicle to hit
an inland city in the United States and they haven't proven that.

Could they—if they were allowed to have a peaceful space program, would that give them all of the excuse necessary to do the testing to develop intercontinental ballistic missiles and reentry systems?

Mr. KLINGNER. Yes. In agreement. They have tested a thermonuclear device, that the size of the seismic event was such that it could only have been through a thermonuclear.

Most assessments are that they have—the missile delivery systems for nuclear weapons against South Korea and Japan. They have demonstrated the ICBM that can reach all the way down to Florida and beyond.

The question is since they haven't demonstrated but that doesn't mean they don't have a reentry vehicle that would——

Mr. SHERMAN. And they haven't tested to be sure that they have the reentry vehicle, but you can smuggle a nuclear weapon.

Now, they're producing a certain number of new nuclear weapons, atomic and thermonuclear, every year.

At what point will they feel they have the minimum they need to defend themselves and will they feel free to sell a nuclear weapon to anybody who's got a billion or two?

Mr. Green. Dr. Green.

Mr. GREEN. In March 2003, I was in negotiations in Beijing with the North Koreans where they told us that if we didn't end our hostile policy and give them what they wanted, they would transfer their nuclear capability.

And then you will recall——

Mr. SHERMAN. Well, they did transfer the capability to Syria or Syria/Iran that Israel destroyed in 2007.

Mr. GREEN. That's right. They followed up on that threat.

Mr. SHERMAN. And they could go forward and—when will they have enough weapons so that they feel that they can transfer fissile material?

Mr. GREEN. They have enough weapons probably so that they can afford to transfer weapons or fissile material without significantly reducing their own military capability.

The question is will they be deterred. I think the answer is yes. It's an excellent question because I think the North Koreans will put more pressure on us by threatening transfer, and we need to have very clear red lines and interdiction capabilities, which is one more reason why sanctions have to be vigorously enforced.

Mr. SHERMAN. So far the Chinese have not agreed that they would prohibit nonstop flights between Tehran and Pyongyang. If those flights stopped in Beijing for fuel, then they would only carry the materials that China agreed to allow.

But if they go nonstop they'll have whatever they have on them. I believe I've gone into overtime. I will yield back.

Mr. YOHO. Thank you. I appreciate the second round.

Let me ask you, in your opinion how much cooperation do you feel China has earnestly afforded to this process as far as sanction compliance?

Any thoughts?

Mr. KLINGNER. I think it has been better than in the past but it's not as much as the U.S. would like. A lot of it, especially from the outside of government, it's hard to get information on how strictly they have implemented sanctions.

I think, since the January 2016 nuclear test, China has allowed better U.N. resolutions than in the past. I think they have stepped up their sanctions enforcement, as they periodically did in the past.

It seems that this sanctions enforcement is, I think, stronger and longer than previous ones. But we also, at the same time, get conflicting reports about economic activity going on near the North Korean border as we even get reports about economic activity being restricted. So I——

Mr. YOHO. Does anybody else have a different opinion?

Mr. GREEN. Just a bit more detail. I understand from international relief organizations that when they try to transfer medicines or other things across the Chinese-North Korean border they're being stopped if there's any metal of any kind.

So the Chinese were implementing pretty strictly up until recently. But since the summit was announced, we have Japanese photographs of Chinese ships helping transfer oil and so on and so forth, and the pattern for China has been they will put economic pressure on North Korea to get North Korea to the table, and as soon as there's a process the Chinese back way off and we can see that coming with a Xi-Kim dialogue going on right now. That's what we have to watch out for.

Mr. YOHO. Well, and that was one of my questions I wanted to ask you. Do you have any factual information that China relaxed the sanctions after the Kim-Xi meetings?

Mr. Denmark, you were going to say something too?

Mr. DENMARK. There's indications that they have dialled it back. I would add to what Dr. Green said, that North Korea—excuse me, China does reduce economic sanctions enforcement after a meeting.

They also put pressure on North Korea when they feel it helps keep the United States on the diplomatic path. So I actually think the Trump administration deserves a great deal of credit for getting the Chinese to enforce sanctions more than they had done before.

That said, China—my sense is that China is already starting to soften its enforcement. My expectation is that they'll continue to soften and my concern, of course, is that the era of maximum pressure is over and we are in different period now than we were before.

Mr. YOHO. Yes, and I have nightmares of snap back with the JCPOA—immediate snap back, which we knew was never going to happen.

But I think this will be different. The thing that—I guess I am concerned about is North Korean vessels—since the summit we are seeing North Korean vessels transport coal and other minerals have been spotted at Chinese harbors.

Chinese officials have stated that China will continue enforcing sanctions but have also suggested lifting U.N. sanctions on North Korea following the summit.

I think this is a huge mistake. This is something that we are going to express our concerns here from this committee and the full committee.

This is something that has brought us to the table to start the negotiations and we cannot back off and I think the President and Secretary Pompeo have articulated that very well and we want to make sure those tools stay in the arsenal as we talked about before this hearing.

There is the saying—it's Korean—that says a job begun is a job half done. The summit happened. We can't go further if we didn't start.

So let's just hope we have wise leaders, that we have the back-bone, I think, or the political willingness to hold people account-able, because this is a historic moment—that if we can bring peace to that peninsula, finally, after the end of the Korean conflict, it'll be a historic moment that the world will be better off for that.

And so let's just hope with the recommendations that you all have afforded us and we appreciate that, that we move in that di-rection.

With that, this hearing is concluded, and I appreciate your pa-tience and everybody in the audience being here.

Thank you.

[Whereupon, at 3:39 p.m., the committee was adjourned.]

APPENDIX

SUBCOMMITTEE HEARING NOTICE
COMMITTEE ON FOREIGN AFFAIRS
U.S. HOUSE OF REPRESENTATIVES
WASHINGTON, DC 20515-6128

Subcommittee on Asia and the Pacific
Ted Yoho (R-FL), Chairman

June 13, 2018

TO: MEMBERS OF THE COMMITTEE ON FOREIGN AFFAIRS

You are respectfully requested to attend an OPEN hearing of the Committee on Foreign Affairs, to be held by the Subcommittee on Asia and the Pacific in Room 2172 of the Rayburn House Office Building (and available live on the Committee website at http://www.ForeignAffairs.house.gov):

DATE: Wednesday, June 20, 2018

TIME: 2:00 p.m.

SUBJECT: The Trump-Kim Summit: Outcomes and Oversight

WITNESSES: Mr. Bruce Klingner
Senior Research Fellow for Northeast Asia
Asian Studies Center
The Heritage Foundation

Michael J. Green, Ph.D.
Senior Vice President for Asia
Japan Chair
Center for Strategic and International Studies

Mr. Abraham Denmark
Director
Asia Program
The Woodrow Wilson International Center for Scholars

By Direction of the Chairman

COMMITTEE ON FOREIGN AFFAIRS

MINUTES OF SUBCOMMITTEE ON _______________*Asia and the Pacific*_______________ HEARING

Day___*Wednesday*___Date___*June 20, 2018*___Room___2172___

Starting Time___*2:00 pm*___Ending Time___*3:40 pm*___

Recesses_____ (____to____) (____to____) (____to____) (____to____) (____to____) (____to____)

Presiding Member(s)

Chairman Yoho

Check all of the following that apply:

Open Session ☑
Executive (closed) Session ☐
Televised ☐

Electronically Recorded (taped) ☐
Stenographic Record ☐

TITLE OF HEARING:

The Trump-Kim Summit: Outcomes and Oversight

SUBCOMMITTEE MEMBERS PRESENT:

Rep. Rohrabacher, Rep. Kinzinger, Rep. Perry, Rep. Wagner, Rep. Chabot
Rep. Sherman, Rep. Bera, Rep. Connolly, Rep. Gabbard, Rep. Titus

NON-SUBCOMMITTEE MEMBERS PRESENT: *(Mark with an * if they are not members of full committee.)*

HEARING WITNESSES: Same as meeting notice attached? Yes ☑ No ☐
(If "no", please list below and include title, agency, department, or organization.)

STATEMENTS FOR THE RECORD: *(List any statements submitted for the record.)*

Letter submitted for the record - Sherman

TIME SCHEDULED TO RECONVENE___________
or
TIME ADJOURNED___*3:40 pm*___

____
Subcommittee Staff Associate

Congress of the United States
Washington, DC 20515

Rec'd TREAS
EXEC SEC

August 2, 2017

The Honorable Rex W. Tillerson
Secretary
U.S. Department of State
Washington, D.C. 20520

The Honorable Steven Mnuchin
Secretary
U.S. Department of the Treasury
Washington, D.C. 20220

Dear Secretary Tillerson and Secretary Mnuchin:

North Korea's recent test of an Intercontinental Ballistic Missile allegedly capable of
reaching Los Angeles, Denver, or Chicago shows the growing severity of the situation on
the Korean peninsula. We must now use every tool available to constrain the Kim regime,
including the targeting of the Chinese businesses that provide the necessary hard currency
for the Kim regime's illicit weapons programs.

We applaud your listing of the Bank of Dandong and others as a primary money laundering
concern pursuant to Section 311 of the USA PATRIOT Act. We hope this listing will send
a strong message to others that facilitating North Korea's illicit weapons program will be
met with significant punishment.

We write to draw your attention to the 2017 report of the United Nations Panel of Experts
(U.N. Panel) monitoring compliance with sanctions against North Korea. This detailed and
credible report adds to the extensive evidence that China's banking industry has failed to
comply with its obligations under U.N. resolutions,[1] and with U.S. sanctions and money
laundering laws.

As you know, those concerns strike at the heart of the purposes of the North Korea
Sanctions and Policy Enhancement Act (NKSPEA), P.L.114-122, which Congress passed
last year by an overwhelming and bipartisan vote. Therefore, we are writing pursuant to
section 102(a) of this law as part of our oversight responsibility to ensure the NKSPEA's
strict and speedy implementation.

Appendix A to this letter is a list of North Korean banks that have been designated by the
United Nations and that have recently accessed our financial system. We respectfully
request a list of all U.N. member states where these banks and their agents continue to
operate, a description of your diplomatic and law enforcement efforts to obtain the
expulsion of these banks' representatives and the freezing of their assets, a list of persons
that knowingly facilitate their operation, and a statement as to whether you intend to
designate these persons under section 104 of the NKSPEA or seek a waiver under section
208.

---

[1] *See* United Nations Security Council resolutions (UNSCR) 1718, 1874, 2087, 2094, 2270 and 2321.

Appendix B to this letter contains a list of North Korean banks that are designated by the U.S. Treasury Department, and that may seek to access our financial system through deceptive financial practices. Please describe your plan to hire the staff described in section 102(b) of the NKSPEA to enforce our laws against those who help North Korean banks access the financial system.

Appendix C contains a list of North Korean banks that are not designated by either the United Nations or the Treasury Department, but which the Panel's report implicated in violations of U.N. sanctions.[2] Please notify us whether you plan to designate these banks under section 104 of the NKSPEA or seek a waiver under section 208.

Appendix D contains a list of Chinese banks that may have provided North Korean banks with correspondent banking services since such services were prohibited under U.N. resolutions.[3] Please describe your efforts to fully enforce the Treasury Department regulation at 31 C.F.R. § 1010.659 and to ensure strict compliance with their Know-Your-Customer, Suspicious Activity reporting, and Anti-Money Laundering compliance obligations with respect to these and other North Korean entities and nationals.

Finally, please provide a list of foreign and domestic financial institutions that maintain direct or indirect correspondent relationships with North Korean banks in violation of U.N. resolutions[4] and U.S. law,[5] and of all member states that have failed to expel these banks' representatives with regard to each of the banks in these appendices.

We thank you for your attention to these issues and look forward to your reply.

Sincerely,

TED S. YOHO, D.V.M.
Chairman
Subcommittee on Asia and the Pacific

BRAD SHERMAN
Ranking Member
Subcommittee on Asia and the Pacific

---

[2] North Korean banks may not operate foreign branches or joint ventures. UNSCR 2270, para. 33.
[3] See Id.; United States v. All Funds in the Accounts of Blue Sea Business Funds, Ltd., et al., No. 16-1954 (D.N.J., Verified Complaint for Civil Forfeiture, filed Sept. 26, 2016, https://www.justice.gov/opa/file/897051/download).
[4] UNSCR 2270, para. 33.
[5] See 31 C.F.R. § 1010.569 (2016).

Appendix A[6]

North Korean Banks That Have Been Designated by the United Nations and by the U.S. Treasury Department

Name	Also Known As/Frequently Known As	Designated under EO
Bank of East Land	AKA: Dongbang Bank, Tongbang Bank, Haedong Bank	13551 19 Apr 2011
Daedong Credit Bank	AKA: DCB Finance Ltd.; FKA: Perigrine-Daesong Development Bank	13382 27 Jun 2013
Korea Kwangson Banking Corp	FKA: Korea Kwangson Finance Company	13382 11 Aug 2009
Amroggang Development Bank	n/a	13382 23 Oct 2009
Korea Daesong Bank	AKA: Daesong Bank, Taesong Bank, Chosen Taesong Unhaeng	13551 18 Nov 2010
Foreign Trade Bank of the D.P.R. of Korea[7]	AKA: Mooyokbank, Korea Trade Bank	13382 11 Mar 2013

Appendix B

North Korean Banks That are Designated by the U.S. Treasury Department, and That May Seek to Access our Financial System Through Deceptive Financial Practices

Name	AKA/FKA	Designated under EO
Koryo Credit Development Bank	FKA: Koryo Global Trust Bank, Koryo-Global Credit Bank	13722 2 Dec 2016
North East Asia Bank	n/a	13772 2 Dec 2016
Koryo Bank	n/a	13772 2 Dec 2016
Kumgang Bank	Possible AKA: Kumgang Export and Import Bank	13772 2 Dec 2016
Tanchon Commercial Bank	FKA: Changgwang Credit Bank; FKA: Korea Changgwang Credit Banking Corporation	13382 11 Mar 2013
Rason International Commercial Bank	n/a	13772 2 Dec 2016
Korea United Development Bank	FKA: Myohyangsan Bank, Myonghyangsan Bank	13772 16 Mar 2016

---

[6] U.N. member states are obligated to freeze the assets of these banks, expel their representatives, close their offices, and deny them any financial services. UNSCR 1718 (2006), para. 8(d); UNSCR 2094, paras. 8 & 11; UNSCR 2270, paras. 15 & 32; & UNSCR, 2321, para. 3.

[7] United States v. $1,071,251.44 of Funds Associated with Mingzheng International, No. 17-01166 (D.D.C., Verified Complaint for Civil Forfeiture filed June 14, 2017).

<u>**Appendix C**</u>
North Korean Banks That are not Designated by either the United Nations or the Treasury Department, but Which the Panel Implicated in Violations of U.N. Sanctions

Institution	AKA/FKA	Basis for investigation or designation
Central Bank of the D.P.R. of Korea	n/a	North Korea's bank of issue; sells gold, which subjects it to mandatory designation under NKSPEA § 104(a).
Chinese Commercial Bank, Rason	n/a	Joint venture; also provides support for trade with North Korea contrary to UNSCR 2321, para. 32.
Credit Bank of Korea	AKA: Korea Credit Bank FKA: International Credit Bank	Associated with Heavy Industry Department of the Korean Workers' Party and should be investigated for possible involvement in the armaments industry.
First Credit Bank	FKA: Kyongyong Credit Bank, Pyongyang	"Possible" joint venture according to the U.N. Panel.
First Eastern Bank, Rason	n/a	Joint venture; involved in mining, a sector sanctioned under EO 13722; involved in exporting gold to the U.S. in possible violation of EO 13570; has foreign branch in Yanbian, China.
First Trust Bank Corporation	AKA: Cheil Credit Bank AKA: Jeil Credit Bank	Joint venture.
Golden Triangle Bank, Namsan	AKA: Golden Delta Bank	Provides support for trade with North Korea in violation of UNSCR 2321, para. 32.
Haedong Bank	n/a	Suspected alias of Bank of East Land, designated by the U.N. and the U.S. Treasury Department.
Hana Banking Corporation	AKA: Hwaryo Bank AKA: Huali Bank AKA: Gorgeous Bank of North Korea FKA: Brilliance Banking Corporation, Ltd	Joint venture.
Hi-Fund Bank International Consortium Bank (ICB)	AKA: Sungri Hi-Fund Int'l Bank; International Consortium Bank	Joint venture; foreign branch of a North Korean bank.
International Bank of Martial Arts, Pyongyang	n/a	Joint venture.
Korea Joint Bank, Pyongyang	AKA: Korea Joint Operation Bank AKA: Chosun Joint Operation Bank	Joint venture.
Koryo Commercial Bank	AKA: Korea Commercial Bank	Joint venture bank established by North Korea and U.S. residents.
Kumgyo International Commercial Bank	n/a	Joint venture.
Orabank	n/a	Joint venture and possible affiliate of North Korea's Foreign Trade Bank, designated under EO 13382.
Ryugyong Commercial Bank	n/a	Suspected front for Daedong Credit Bank, designated by the U.N. and the U.S., operates in Beijing.

<u>**Appendix D**</u>
Chinese Banks That May Have Provided North Korean Banks with Indirect Correspondent
Banking Services Since Such Services Were Prohibited Under U.N. Resolutions, Identified
in United States v. All Funds in the Accounts of Blue Sea Business Funds, Ltd., et al., No.
16-1954 (D.N.J., Verified Complaint for Civil Forfeiture, filed Sept. 26, 2016)

- Agricultural Bank of China
- Bank of Communications Co. of China
- Bank of Dalian
- Bank of Dandong
- Bank of Jinzhou
- China Construction Bank

- China Merchants Bank
- China Minsheng Banking Corporation
- Guangdong Development Bank
- Hua Xia Bank
- Industrial & Commercial Bank of China
- Shanghai Pudong Development Bank